The Pulaski Reader

Translated and Compiled by

Peter Obst

The Pulaski Reader
Cover art by Gabriela Paciorek. Used with permission of the Polish Heritage Society of Philadelphia
This edition published in 2021

Winged Hussar is an imprint of

Winged Hussar Publishing, LLC
1525 Hulse Rd, Unit 1
Point Pleasant, NJ 08742

Copyright © Winged Hussar Publishing
ISBN 978-1-950423-64-4 PB
ISBN 978-1-950423-85-9 EB
LCN 2021950212

Bibliographical References and Index
1. History. 2. Poland. 3. American Revolution

Winged Hussar Publishing, LLC All rights reserved
For more information
Visit us at www.wingedhussarpublishing.com

Twitter: WingHusPubLLC
Facebook: Winged Hussar Publishing LLC

BOOK INSTITUTE

©POLAND

This publication has been supported by the © POLAND Translation Program

***Dedicated to Edward Pinkowski**
Historian, Scholar and Polish-American
Founder of the Poles in America Foundation*

Table of Contents

Translator's Note

The "Rogowski Memoirs" is perhaps one of the most fascinating books I have had the privilege to translate. It is full of vivid events told in a quirky "old Polish" that could have only been spoken by an authentic eighteenth-century Polish nobleman, but it is also totally inaccurate as an historical record. Therefore, it can only be looked upon as an entertaining tale, not as a source for factual information about Pulaski's life.

The whole is structured as a memoir, a format that since has become a cliche among writers of Polish historical fiction who claim with the utmost sincerity that their works are based on a long-lost diary that they have come across on a dusty shelf in along abandoned manor.

In this case the incidents seem to fit what might have been Pulaski's life except that in several cases the actual circumstances are known from authoritative or verifiable sources, and these do not match up with the story as presented by Rogowski.

To give his hero more authenticity, Gaszynski has Rogowski slip-in mention that Americans had a lot of trouble pronouncing his names, disfiguring his into Kokoski or even Kolkoski - possibly to create the impression that Rogowski was really there, because there was an actual Kotowski who is listed on the rolls of the Pulaski Legion.

It would have been wonderful if this had been an authentic memoir, because of the terrific details, yet we know from various sources that Pulaski landed in Massachusetts not on the Chesapeake Bay, and that he first met Washington at Moland House in Bucks County, not at Brandywine.

So please read and enjoy this memoir for the stimulation of your imagination as things might have been, not to provide the actual historical frame for Pulaski's exploits.

Peter J. Obst, October 2021

Casimir Pułaski's Life 1745-1779 - Timeline

1745

6 Mar. - Casimir Pułaski is born in Warsaw at the Pulaski residence on the corner of Nowy Swiat and Warecka Streets. He is the second son (of three) born to the Starosta of Warka, Józef Pulaski and Marianna Zielinska his wife.

1762

Leaves the Theatine School in Warsaw and becomes a page at the courts of Prince Charles of Courland [Kurlandia]; and Semigallia, son of King Augustus III.

1763

Pułaski gains his first military experience during a six-month long siege at Prince Charles' military camp, during the siege of the capital of Courland - Mitava (now Jelgava in the Latvian Republic) by the Russian Army.

1764

Sept. - Józef Pulaski and his three sons take part in the election of Stanislaus Augustus Poniatowski as King of Poland in Warsaw

1767

Dec. - Józef Pulaski and his three sons leave Warsaw for Winiary, and start organizing an armed uprising in south-eastern Poland

1768

Franciszek and Casimir Pulaski travel along the Dniester River recruiting for the confederation whose political side was being prepared at that time in Lvov by their father.

29 Feb. - The establishment of the Bar Confederation in Podole with the Chamberlain of Rozan, Michal Krasinski, at its head.

4 Mar. - The establishment of the military arm of the confederation with Józef Pulaski at its head with the title of Marshal of the Union; among the commanders of the regiments were his three sons, Franciszek, Starosta of Augustów; Casimir, Starosta of Zezuliniec; and Antoni, Starosta of Czeresz

Circa 20 Apr. - Casimir leads his first skirmish with the vanguard of the Russian troops which had been sent to Podole to put down the uprising.

23 April - Casimir defends Starokonstantynów

May - Casimir fights defensive actions near Chmielnik and Winnica and then fortifies Berdyczów. After a two-week siege he capitulates. He and his troops are taken prisoner by the Russians.

20 June - The Russian army captures the town of Bar, the second important insurgent stronghold; Józef Pulaski crosses the Dniester River with the rest of his troops and takes refuge on Turkish soil.

17 July - Casimir Pulaski is freed by the Russians and goes to the Bar Confederation camp at Chocim.

Sept - Oct - Casimir and his brothers carry out raids along the northern bank of the Dniester River.

Dec. - Józef Pulaski is arrested by the Turks because of intrigues in the confederate camp

1769

Winter - The Pulaski brothers at the head of their troops occupy and fortify Zwaniec and the Holy Trinity Trenches on the Dniester River.

Feb. - Casimir Pulaski carries out a reconnaissance raid toward Zaleszczyki and fights a skirmish near Tluste; at the same time receives a declaration from the confederates of western Little Poland (Malopolska) to join them.

Early March - Antoni Pulaski is captured by Russian troops

8 March - The Russian army takes Zwaniec and the Holy Trinity Trenches; Franciszek and Casimir Pulaski take refuge along with the survivors on the southern shore of the Dniestr River, on Turkish soil

End March - Casimir Pulaski crosses the frontier in Kuty and marches through Czarnohora and Gorgany towards the Kraków region.

Mid-April - Józef Pulaski, dies in a Turkish prison as a result of a raging epidemic.

Late April - Franciszek Pulaski returns with his units to Poland and appears in eastern Little Poland.

Circa 13 May - The Pulaski brothers meet in Sambor and decide to operate in unison.

22 May - Franciszek Pulaski is named marshal of the confederated Przemysl region.

End May - The Pulaski brothers take part in an unsuccessful attempt to occupy Lvov.

Late June - Arriving in the Lublin area and reaching Polesie, the brothers organize a rising in Lithuania.

6 July - Casimir Pulaski is victorious in the battle at Kukielki.

12 July Casimir Pulaski is victorious in the battle at Slonim

3 Aug - Casimir Pulaski is named Marshal of the confederation forces in the Lomza region.

13 Sept. - The detachments led by the Pulaski brothers are defeated at Orzechów and Franciszek is killed in battle.

Sept. - Casimir Pulaski takes part in the war council at Zborov in Slovakia which precedes the establishment of the General High Board of the Confederation called the Generality which becomes the chief insurgent authority

1770

13 Jan. - Casimir Pulaski is wounded in the hand during a skirmish near Grab.

15 May - Pulaski loses a battle near Pilzno during a raid in the direction of Kraków.

Mid-June - Austrian authorities had granted asylum to the Generality while at Presov in Slovakia. Pulaski met with the Austrian Emperor Joseph II who visited the confederates.

3 Aug. - Pulaski loses a battle at Wysowa with Drewitz's army, and later takes shelter on Austrian soil

7 Aug. - Pulaski meets in Zborov with Charles Dumouriez, the new French government emissary and military adviser to the Generality

1 Sept. - Night raid on Kraków after which he retreats toward Częstochowa

9 Sept. - Occupies the monastery at Jasna Góra (Częstochowa)

29 Sept - Organizes a raid from Zarnowiec through Jedrzejów to Koniecpol

19 Oct. - Raids from Częstochowa towards Poznan

Nov. - Prepares Jasna Góra for a siege, the Russian army approaches Częstochowa twice in this period

31 Dec. - The beginning of the siege of Częstochowa by the army of General Drewitz, supported by Prussian artillery

1771

4 Jan - Casimir Pulaski organizes a raid from the monastery and destroys an enemy battery

9 Jan - An all-out attack on Częstochowa is repulsed

15 Jan. - Drewitz army leaves Częstochowa

Circa 1 Mar. - Pulaski stages a raid from Częstochowa toward Krasnik

21 May - Starts a raid through Tymbark, Limanowa, Nowy Sacz, Debica, Zamosc (skirmishing along the way in Kolbuszowa, Debica, Mielec);

2 June - Pulaski's units fight battle with a Russian army corps at Zamosc after which they retreat towards Tarnów and Lanckorona

18 June - Casimir Pulaski is back at Jasna Góra which is again threatened with a siege by Drewitz and the Polish Royal Army under the command of Branicki

20 Oct. - Leaves Częstochowa for a diversionary raid in the direction of Warsaw; meanwhile a group commanded by Strawinski was to make an attempt to abduct King Stanislaus August Poniatowski

31 Oct. - He loses a battle at Skaryszew near Radom; is wounded in the arm and his scattered units retreat towards Częstochowa

3 Nov. - The abduction of King Stanislaus August Poniatowski proves unsuccessful, Pulaski is implicated as an instigator of the scheme.

30 Nov. - Austrian authorities forbid Pulaski entry into Austria as one of the organizers of the attempted abduction of the king

1772

Circa 20 Feb. - Stages a raid from Częstochowa towards Kraków

31 May - Pulaski leaves the Jasna Góra fortress and takes refuge in Prussian Silesia

End June - Arrives in Dresden

Aug - Visits Altwasser in Silesia under the assumed name of Rudzinski to see Franciszka Krasinska and then surreptitiously watches the maneuvers of the Prussian troops near Nysa

Sept. - Leaves Germany and stops in Nancy, France.

1773

March - Casimir Pulaski moves to Paris

Begin May - Goes to Dresden to be nearer Poland while the trial of the participants in the abduction attempt is being held

7 June - At the beginning of the trial (which lasts until 28 August) with Casimir Pulaski sentenced in absentia to beheading for attempted regicide

25 Sept. - Under the assumed name of Korwin he meets with the leaders of the Generality in Strasbourg and announces that he will take part in the war between Turkey and Russia, after which he travels to Paris

1774

Mar. - Leaves Paris and with a group of companions goes to Turkey

12 Apr. - Sails from Venice to Ragusa (Dubrovnik) in order to reach the Turkish army which is fighting the Russians at the mouth of the Danube River

Circa 20 June - Reaches the Vizier's camp near Shumen west of Varna where he takes part in the defeat suffered by the Turkish forces
Circa 15 Oct - After the unsuccessful Turkish expedition and a three-month long journey (Adrianople, Constantinople, Izmir) he returns to France and stops in Marseilles

20 Dec. - Józef Zajaczek writes a memorial to the French authorities to obtain financial aid for Pulaski

1775

Oct - Living in Marseilles living from an allowance and loans and spends a short time in debtors' prison

1776

15 Aug - Appeals to the Sejm (Polish Parliament) in Warsaw to be allowed to return to Poland but there is no reply; at this time that he makes efforts to be accepted into the American Revolutionary Army

1777

Mar – Apr - Arrives in Paris after obtaining permission to go to America

29 May - Receives a letter of recommendation from Benjamin Franklin addressed to George Washington

6 June - Writes a letter of farewell to his sister Anne in Warsaw and sails on the ship Massachusetts from Nantes to America
23 Jul - Lands in America at Marblehead near Boston

Aug - After a short stay in Boston he reports at the HQ of George Washington located in Moland House in Warwick Township, Bucks County, Pennsylvania

24 Aug - Offers his military services to Congress

11 Sept - Takes part in his first battle on American soil, on the Brandywine Creek between Chester and Philadelphia

15 Sept - Named a General of Cavalry for the Continental Army

3 October - Fights at Germantown and covers Washington's retreat after the battle is lost.

Nov – Dec - Pulaski patrols the area around Valley Forge where Washington's army takes up winter quarters; his own quarters are in Devault Beaver's house

1778

8 Jan - Moves with his unit to Trenton where he organizes and trains the troops.

End Feb – Beg. Mar. - Joins General Wayne in the fighting against the British in New Jersey; a skirmish at Haddonfield.

March - While in Valley Forge Pulaski asks Washington to release him from his post as the commander of cavalry and puts forward a plan for an independent detachment which he would command.

19 Mar - Presents a plan of forming a Legion to Congress while staying at Yorktown.

28 Mar - Receives Congressional permission to form a legion of cavalry and infantry.

Late Apr - Establishes the headquarters of the Legion in Baltimore.

18 May - Pulaski's Legion receives its banner; embroidered by the Moravian Order of Sisters of Bethlehem.

15 Sept - Pulaski reports to Washington that the Legion is ready for action.

8 Oct - Pulaski's Legion arrives at Egg Harbor where a week later it was surprised by a British night attack and suffered serious losses.

24 Oct - The Legion arrives at Trenton, then relocates to Sussex Court House and finally to Minisink where it is ordered to defend the colonists against the Native Americans.

15 Nov - Pulaski asks Washington to be released from his post and writes of his intention to return to Europe.

1779

Jan - While in Philadelphia he withdraws the resignation he sent to Congress.

8 Feb - Washington orders the Legion to march south from Yorktown in the direction of Savannah.

8 May - The Legion arrives in Charleston where it takes part in the fighting for the town.

19 Aug - Pulaski's last letter to Congress.

14 Sept - Pulaski's Legion arrives at Savannah, to take part in taking the town.

9 Oct - Pulaski is mortally wounded in the attack on Savannah.

15 Oct - Dies on board the brigantine Wasp while it is still anchored near Savannah; his body is taken to nearby Greenwich Plantation and buried there in a torchlight ceremony.

21 Oct - A symbolic funeral of the hero in Charleston.

1793

Through the efforts of Antoni Pulaski the Sejm (Polish Parliament) revokes the sentence from the trial held in 1773 (in absentia) which found Pulaski guilty of attempted regicide and condemned him to death.

1825

A corner stone is laid for Casimir Pulaski's monument by Lafayette in Savannah's Chippewa Square.

1855

A monument to Pulaski designed by Robert Launitz is finally erected in Monterey Square in Savannah. The corner stone from Chippewa Square and Pulaski's remains from Greenwich Plantation are placed in its underground brick lined crypt.

1910

Casimir Pulaski's monument in Washington is unveiled.

1929

A monument to Pulaski is unveiled in Krynica, Poland; it is the first monument to Pulaski built on Polish soil.

1967

The Casimir Pulaski museum in Warka-Winiary, Poland opens.

1979

On the 200th anniversary of Pulaski's death, a statue by Kazimerz Danilewicz, a gift of the Polish nation to the United States, is dedicated in Buffalo, and a copy placed in the park near the Pulaski museum in Warka.

1996

The Pulaski Monument in Savannah is taken down for renovation, the underground crypt is uncovered and found to contain two cornerstones and an iron box. The box bears a plate "Brigadier General Casimer Pulaski" and contains the bones of a man matching Pulaski in stature and physical characteristics.

1997

A conference is convened on Pulaski at the Museum in Warka, Poland; among those delivering papers is Edward Pinkowski

RESZTY PAMIĘTNIKÓW

MACIEJA ROGOWSKIEGO

ROTMISTRZA KONFEDERACYI BARSKIÉJ.

POPRZEDZONE PRZEDMOWĄ I WYDANE

PRZEZ

KONSTANTEGO GASZYŃSKIEGO.

WYDANIE TRZECIE.

LWÓW.

NAKŁADEM KSIĘGARNI

GUBRYNOWICZA I SCHMIDTA

1888.

The Remainder of the Memoirs of Maciej Rogowski Regimental Captain of the Bar Confederation

Published with an introduction by

Konstanty Gaszynski

Third Edition

Gubrynowicz and Schmidt

Lwów, 1888

Introduction by the Publisher

Nearly thirty years ago, as a far as I can remember, there lived in the neighborhood of my parents' home a very illustrious citizen, Maciej Rogowski. He was known in the area as the *Captain of Cavalry*; during the Bar Confederation he had this rank and fought during this five year war. It was considered a rebellion against the Court of King Stanislaw August and the supporters of the Tsarina in Petersburg, but every true Pole knew that it was a holy fight for the rights of the nation. Rogowski was also called an American, for the reason that he went to that remote part of the world with Pulaski and Kosciuszko, and several other Poles, to fight for American independence under Washington's command.

All respected and loved Mr. Maciej because he was friendly and kind, fun loving and joyful. He saw much of the world, met many people, saw much and had experiences. His talk, therefore, was incredibly interesting and the stories were often laced with humorous anecdotes which were always entertaining to hear. For fifteen miles around, at every name-day party, baptism or wedding among the nobility it was unthinkable not to invite the *Captain*. And when a party was planned in the neighborhood, everyone would ask, "Will the American be there?"

The memories of one's youth do not fade easily, so today after so many years, I still can picture the figure of this respected old gentleman clearly and distinctly, as if I had just seen him yesterday. Rogowski wore the old traditional nobleman's attire: a split-sleeve coat, a brocade robe and a woven sash. He was slender and tall, straight like a young man despite his advanced age and bad health. His mustache was long and white as milk, hanging down his thin face, giving seriousness to his animated face that was lit up by large blue eyes. Across his bald head there were scars and traces of old wounds. And many times, while drinking he would repeat jokingly that his head was strong - because it had been riveted with lead and steel. Rogowski never married and for this reason he was proud of his title of *March Cavalier* [word play on bachelor/ cavalry captain]. His older sister, a childless widow, kept house for him.

On returning back home after a long absence the *Captain* found that his family's village was deserted and nearly ruined. There were debts, so he sold it and gathering some capital, had to live on rental income and loans. But in time with good husbandry, he set himself up and did well enough; he was not wealthy but did not know want. He could entertain guests, especially on the Day of St. Maciej [Matthew], which celebration usually turned into a three-day revel. From this the neighbors would depart well fed and - more often than not - quite drunk. But in this last instance their host would console them with the old Polish proverb, the noble sentiment, that only a dishonest man fears to get tipsy *for while intoxicated he might speak of his own dishonorable acts and treasonous intents.*

Though my father was younger, he lived in great friendship with the *Captain.* They visited often, and when I was a young boy, I listened to their long conversations with interest and enjoyment. Rogowski spoke of the Bar Confederation, while my father talked about Kosciuszko's Insurrection. And in this fashion, I learned the history of our nation, beginning not with Lech, [legendary founder of Poland] but with King Stanislaw August. To me, Casimir Pulaski and Thaddeus Kosciuszko were the greatest of Polish heroes, because I knew about them since childhood and learned their biographies from eyewitnesses who accompanied these great leaders.

Rogowski had a great book bound in red satin, in which he wrote down his entire life, the wars and voyages. When asked, he would fetch the book from his office and read parts of it. These stories were listened to in silence and praised at conclusion. Later, when I was older, I would come from Warsaw to vacation at home and started to write poetry and prose, I'd sneak off to Raducz[1], to see Rogowski, who loved me greatly, and borrow French and Polish books from him. He would sometimes let me read from that great red volume. The title of it was: *A recounting of incidents in which during my youth I took part or witnessed.*

In 1828 Rogowski died, his sister gave the rental property to others selling the livestock and possessions, then moved to live with relatives in Kujavia[2]. For a time, everyone remembered the old *Captain* with sympathy, then as it is with people, the talk ceased. Even I must admit that I forgot my old friend and his book, whose pages once provided me with such great enjoyment.

---

[1] Raducz is a village in the administrative district of Gmina Nowy Kawęczyn, within Skierniewice County, Łódź Voivodeship, in central Poland. It was probably founded in the 18th century.
[2] Kujavia is a historical region in north-central Poland, situated on the left bank of Vistula,

Yet soon there were some more important incidents: the night of November 21, the campaign of 1831[3] and the unhappy emigration that followed. Seeing the country in death throes there was no time to think of dead neighbors. But finally, six or seven years ago I received Pasek's memoirs and other documents on family history published in Poznan from manuscripts by Raczynski. Then I remembered the red-bound book of Captain Rogowski and immediately decided to make every effort to find it and have the original, or even a copy, published in France. Difficulties I encountered spurred me on and made me firm in my resolve, even more so because there was nothing in print about Casimir Pulaski's stay in Germany, Turkey, France and America. I found nothing in Kitowicz's memoirs, and Ferrand had only one mention, and that of little significance. But I remembered that Rogowski wrote much about these things.

Therefore, I immediately contacted one of my good friends who lived in the Poznan Kingdom and providing him with the necessary instructions as to the place and persons whom he was to see, I urged him strongly that he himself, or through friends, should try to recover this manuscript.

I waited for a few years, as my friend having no relations left in Kujavia. But then growing impatient I started to send numerous letters; he made a special trip to the Kingdom, replying in his letter that he was *a new Argonaut in pursuit of another golden fleece!*

He inquired of Mrs. D., the sister of Rogowski who lived in the vicinity of Kowal with her relations, and explaining the matter, stated that he was asking in my name, a search started through the house for the manuscript. This would be easily recognized for its red cover and was later found on a shelf in the pantry.

> "I grabbed the dusty book (he wrote) lost among the cheeses and vittles with the kind of enthusiasm as was possessed by young Achilles when he snatched weapons from among the feminine baubles where sly Ulysses concealed them. The covers were intact, but unfortunately - *oh, horror, horror* - inside fully half the pages were missing. For the format of the book was large and the paper thick in these Relations so it was used to seal broken windowpanes. And every Easter holiday more damage would be wrought, as it was admitted to

---

[3] The "November Uprising" against Russia in 1831.

me that through ignorance (which proves that ignorance can be a sin) pages of Bar Confederation History were used to line pans for baking cookies and cakes. Most of the pages were missing from the front. However, the housekeeper, obviously not members of the *des bas blues* [upper crust] confraternity, ripped pages from both ends. I had the thought that this rescued middle portion might hold no interest and was not worth taking, but when I looked at it I could not tear myself away from reading. After over an hour of reading I reached the end and was truly sorry there was not more. In that which remained after the barbarous havoc wrought by the illiterate hand, there were many interesting and little-known details that could be historical material and also a picture of customs during those times. With permission of Mrs. D. I took your treasure and kept it with me. I have it here in secret, copying it onto thinner paper in a portable format, and when the opportunity presents itself, I will send this to you in Paris."

The letter slowly saddened me. How many historical treasures (I thought) gathered by our forebears suffered a similar fate. Fires set by Swedes and Muscovites did consume many interesting manuscripts but the careless fashion of running a household and lack of literary schooling probably caused the loss of many more! I consoled myself with the thought that my efforts saved (after damage in a nobleman's larder) at least half of Rogowski's memoirs. But long was my wait for the expected package, yet at the beginning of the year I received it and now can take to the printer.

The reader will find here the last actions by Pulaski at and his departure from the fortress. Then the story of his first emigration to Germany, which was not unlike our own (at least the bad parts), for there were disagreements, insults, and duels - and even a Prophet. Later, there are interesting details about Pulaski at the head of a Confederate unit during the Turkish war against the Muscovites in 1774. Then his travel through France and arrival in America in 1777. There is mention of his skirmishes with the English where Pulaski and his countrymen fought bravely and gained glory for Polish arms in the world. Finally, a description of the death suffered by this Ajax of Bar during the storming of the City of Savannah at the end of 1779 and the departure of the memoir's author to Europe.

The last part of the manuscript was the most interesting because it may be the only historical document on the subject. There are no Polish or French works where any of these details can be found.[4]

We knew only about the place and date of Casimir Pulaski's death. But of the hardships he endured, the battles he fought, the discouragement he experienced from the time of his landing on the soil of the United States - there is not a word.

On the few pages missing at the end, there must not have been anything interesting, for I know that Captain Rogowski spent nearly ten months ill in bed with a dire sickness during the Kosciuszko Insurrection in 1794. In this new struggle, shorter but more devoted to the national cause, he could have had no part. But we may well regret the loss of the first four books in which, as I remember, there was a detailed account of Pulaski's expedition to Lithuania, the arrival of French officers to aid the Confederation, the taking of the Krakow fortress, and the most detailed information about the long and heroic defense of Częstochowa against attacks launched by Drewicz who, at this place that he called a *hen-house* but lost 2,000 men and from where had to shamefully retreat.

The style of these memoirs is rather naive, sometimes crude, but clear, bright and full of life. The scenes are shown without artistic pretensions yet form dramatic groupings. There are anecdotes, epigrammatic comments, aptly sketched portraits of individuals known from history. Finally, in the writing there something very engaging and reminiscent of Pasek![5]

In our language we do not have that which the French call the military style in which Balzac wrote his *Historie de Napoleon racontee par un vieux soldat*. But we have something great that is analogous: a style that may be called the *nobleman's* or the *split-sleeve coat style* [reference to the traditional nobleman's attire the *kontusz*]. We have some recently published works in this style, set in various eras, by persons who wrote for themselves not for the public. They had no intent of producing artistic styles - they simply related to naive fashion, as if they were sitting at their fireside with a pipe or glass of Hungarian red wine in hand and were telling a story to friends. Among memorials of

---

[4]In only two books published in America: The history of the American revolution, by David Ramsay and the twelve-volume correspondence of Washington collected and published in Boston in 1837; before Jared Sparks - can one find a few short but very favorable remarks about Pulaski's courage and his heroic death.

[5] Jan Pasek's memoirs about the 17th century.

this type, first place is held by Pasek's Memoirs; later there is General Kopec's *Journal of Travels*. Kilinski's *Diaries* and the writings of Rogowski. In many parts of *Pan Tadeusz*, Mickiewicz masterfully seized this type of nobles' language, and preserved it for posterity, cast in the eternal bronze of his rhyme!

This nobleman's style is so commonplace that I will go as far as to say it is not for use in books. For in 1828 or 1829 when Pasek's manuscript was given to an editor at one of the literary magazines in Warsaw, the editor, a man who reveled in the well-bred endings as used by Osinski and the tuneful expressions of Stanislaw Potocki, which were rounded out by Cicero's file - stated that if he were to use parts of it, he would have to invest much time. *For it is a fine and a good thing but the editing and style must be changed from end to end.* Pasek's work was in danger of this kind of sacrilege; and the incredible verses from the seventeenth century were a hairbreadth from being buried in classical mortar applied by a mason of the Warsaw school!

Buffon, though a member of the Paris Academy wrote: *le style c'est l'homme* [the style is the man] but our artisans could not stand individuality. They were the great levelers, saying "style is the echo of our voice, the modulation of the many works we publish stamped by our seal!" Having the military government of Prince Konstantin as an example they wanted to dress writers in the one and same uniform, arrange them in ranks and have them execute maneuvers under one command. Woe to him who should make an error in a movement; he would be shorn of honor and sentenced: *non dignus est intrare...*

People of the old school reached a point where they would even want to beautify and order nature. They clipped the fulsome branches of trees, dressed shepherds in satin, and placed silk ribbons on the necks of sheep.

I am sure that had the Venus Medici not been carved of Carrera marble, but made of wax, and fell into the hands of *Coysevox, Coustou* or another such sculptor from the time of Louis XV, they would have rounded her arms, given her a broader face, and on her head would be placed, if not a wig, then at least a wreath of flowers - and in her hand a freshly blooming rose!

I must apologize to the reader for this romantic sermonizing - I was led to this by considering the danger faced by *Jan Chryzostom Pasek's* work - and spilled my bile *intra parenthesis*, as Rogowski was wont to say. Now to return to the subject.

These *Remains of Memoirs* that I am publishing have this main virtue and thus become interesting from the historical and literary viewpoint, because they have this *nobleman's style* giving us a daguerreotype of a man living in the middle of the past century and looking at the world through glasses tinted by the dust of a Jesuit education and the prejudices of his age. Yet he is one who, from the place where he stands, sees things very simply and clearly. He is not an actor appearing on a stage knowing that a large audience has its eyes upon him. Therefore, he puts on no makeup, he does not use shoe-lifts, nor does he drape his tunic into artistic folds. He relates plainly all the incidents to which he was a witness that were worthy of memory. If the telling is sometimes humorous or dramatic - it is natural without effort to create humor or create an effect. The pen is not an artificial stylus, but the recorder of the everyday speech - a horn which transmits sound without beautifying it.

Today when such a nobleman's tale is to be placed in Guttenberg's form, something never expected to happen, I do not regret the care I endured, nor the troubles and worries that took place over the years during which the manuscript was found and obtained. Persons who are interested in things of their fathers, for whom literary and historical monuments are of higher worth than shares in railroads - will be grateful for the discovery and publication of this surprising story. I myself am happy and have a pride in the thought that there is this edifice to our past, that was built by the dear departed Count Raczynski through his effort and care for today's Poland - and that I added one more small brick to it!

Paris May 30, 1847
Konstanty Gaszynski

General Casimir Pulaski by Jan Styka

The Remainder of the Memoirs of Maciej Rogowski

End of Book Five

Zaremba's Desertion - Incursion by forces of Three Neighboring Powers onto Polish lands - Departure of Casimir Pulaski from Częstochowa

... what alarmed and saddened Pulaski. Because Zaremba, from the skirmish at Koscian (where he totally defeated Captain Olszow as I already mentioned earlier) and the matter of Widawski (where he roughed up Branecki's people) avoided all occasions for battle and did no harm to the enemy — though his going over to the royal side weakened the Confederation and served as a bad example to others. Meanwhile, the awful letter he wrote to Salder put a stain on the national character and tore at the hearts of true patriots.

18.   I must here add *in parenthesis* that Zaremba's command by then had distinguished itself by its strictness and military discipline. There was very little rabble there, all the men were well equipped and trained. So did Zaremba love his army that he tended to conserve it, rarely going into battle. Dzierzanowski, a famous wit, had said that Zaremba "did not want the bright guns to get soot on them from firing; nor the white ammunition belts and brass cartridge boxes to get stained with blood."

Sometime it happened that he could have scattered a small Russian or regular army unit but he let them pass right under his nose, preferring to guard his own villages from Cossack raids or looting by such brigands and robbers like Zbikowski, Bachowski and others (who under the guise of the Confederation plied the trade of highwaymen) than to fight for the endangered faith and independence of the Rzeczpospolita [Poland]. In the man there were very many virtues but private interest spoiled everything as he thought of himself only, and not of the common cause. And that is why now he became submissive to Poniatowski. He got friendly with Salder and bowed to the Russian Tsarina; to save his fortune and obtain rank at the court.

19.   Thus Pulaski, wishing to punish Zaremba's lack of loyalty struck him in the place most vital to him, that is his lands, deciding to burn and destroy completely his properties at Kisiele and Rozprza a few miles from Piotrkow. To achieve this end he took with him about five-hundred men and marched from Częstochowa on June 24 on the feast of St. John the Baptist taking the tract leading to Sieradz. We marched about a mile, when Pulaski passing by my unit beckoned to me (for as it was said already he loved me and shared his thoughts). I gave the horse the spur and caught up with him and we rode on the side discussing things, but mostly about Zaremba's treachery. Pulaski was a lively man and quick to anger, so it was said about him with some truth that his blood would boil on occasion. He was very angry at Zaremba recalling his earlier activities that bode no good for the future. How instead of aiding Częstochowa when it was under siege by Drewicz, he uselessly chased after Malczewski; or how later he would not announce the Proclamation of Dethronement among his command. And then his contacts with the pawns of Warsaw, with the Prussian generals and the Russian colonel's wife Renowa, all with great affection and confidences. I cannot forget how sharp the words were that fell from his lips when he spoke of all these things and could not get over the fact that when Zaremba visited Częstochowa a few months earlier he did not have him arrested and put before a court martial as a plotting traitor (about which there were already rumors.)

20.   After a hurried march we reached Radomsk by evening. It was a small town about six miles from Częstochowa and there we made our camp for the night. Pulaski and Captain Wielichowski (who recently left Zaremba and joined us with his men) and I, made our quarters in a brick home of Stacherski, a jurist. But just as we lay down to rest, with Pulaski in the better furnished room, and Wielichowski and I in the other chamber, we heard a knocking at the door. Then someone entered and started a loud argument. I jumped onto my feet, grabbed a pistol in one hand and sabre in the other and asked through the door as to what the noise was about. Then I heard the voice of a messenger saying that he had brought an urgent letter to the Marshal from Radziminski at Częstochowa and had orders to deliver it immediately. Striking a fire and lighting a candle, I drew back the bolt and opened the door. I recognized the face of our companion Osipowski holding a large letter in his hand. While Wielichowski and I were discussing whether we should wake

Pulaski or wait till dawn, he came awakened by the noise, and entered our room. Then taking the candlestick and the letter, he started to read. Right away we could see that it was not good news because the color in Pulaski's face had started to run out and while reading he began to tap with his foot while twisting his mustache — which indicated consternation. "Rogowski (he told me) have the trumpeter call the men to horse in two hours — we have no time to rest — just don't oversleep, my brother." Then he went to his room and slammed shut the door, leaving the three of us wondering what was happening, which we guessed was nothing good.

21.   Thus, well before sunrise when the squads formed up on the market square, we were most surprised that instead of marching to Piotrkow Pulaski told us to march back to Częstochowa. So Zaremba got away this time but not for long, because God punished him better than could have been accomplished by our sinful hands by burning his mansion and properties. This did not happen right away but a few years later, and I'll mention it here because there will be no opportunity to speak later about his unhappy end. Poniatowski received his submission with joy, but aside from courteous words and promises he gave him no command or any hoped-for favors. On arrival at the capital Zaremba was greeted by catcalls and shouted epithets calling him a traitor. As a deserter, he was pelted with stones and mud. At the court he tried to get into the king's good graces but without avail. With a sour expression on his face he consequently went back to his home in Sieradz where while taking a dry bath he was burned alive. It happened in this way. He was in the wooden tub, closed up to the neck, while through a side opening steam was generated from alcohol that was poured from a ceramic demijohn. The boy handling it, dropped it either accidentally or because it was too heavy. The alcohol spilled partly into the tub, and partly onto the floor and as it broke, upset a candlestick holding a lighted candle. Quickly everything was on fire, the lid of the tub was warped by the heat. There was no way to remove it and free Zaremba who was on fire and screamed to heaven for succor. No one, neither his brother, who was there, nor any of the servants thought to get and axe and smash the tub (which was later done). He was horribly burned and died a few hours later in terrible sufferings. It was also said (but I doubt it) that it was not the alcohol outside that caught fire, but the liquor which was already in his gut and this caused his death. For Zaremba liked strong drink and especially spirits which he imbibed without measure. Like it or not, the

finger of God was in this incident, for here was punished a disloyal man who abandoned friends and went over to the opposite side.

22.   We marched quickly on the same road we used the previous day, thinking and speculating as to the reason for our rapid return. The marshal rode in silence, saddened, and spoke to no one. We were afraid to ask, but later learned the bad new in the letter Osipowski brought. The news were as follows. Radziminski (a fine and courageous cavalryman, whom the marshal would place in command of Częstochowa when he left on one of his raids) told Pulaski that immediately after our departure he was informed that the Austrian [king] at last removed his false mask — chasing out the Generality [Command of the Bar Confederation]. Tyniec, Lanckorona, and Bobrek were occupied by his troops and taken by treacherous means. His forces moved into the Krakow, Sandomierz and Wolyn voivodships, knowing already that the Prussians had moved into Wielkopolska and were after the Confederates. It was impossible to oppose all three powers and now one had to see to one's own safety. Pulaski was accused of regicide, which might cost him his head. Radziminski advised that the marshal forget about punishing Zaremba and think about his own position. All these details were revealed to me a few days later as we stealthily made our way through Silesia — and time proved the truth of it.

23.   Well after sunset we reached Częstochowa and immediately Pulaski conferred with Radziminski, the two having shut themselves in the old refectory where they talked about an hour. I started to undress in my cell for I was most weary after the two-day march when Pulaski come to see me. I was surprised at his appearance for his face was much changed and instead of his rich hussar's uniform decorated with silver (which he always wore) he had on a grey jacket and a plain navy-blue cap with grey fleece trim. "Maciej, (he said to me) our cause is in a bad way. My brother, I have never despaired, but this time when three powers have declared war against us and our allies do nothing, I see no possibility of defense. One could perhaps break down walls with one's head but the head would get broken instead, but I need my head for the future when these bad times pass. What more, if we desperately hang onto this holy place devoted to the Mother of God, it will be ruined and despoiled by Protestants and Schismatics. So I must cross the border to save myself, and knowing how much you love me, and that I may always count on you, I am asking you to accompany me on this trip. "

"My dear Marshal (I was quite touched by this and said, kissing him on the shoulder [?]) I will follow you to the ends of the earth, even to the Antipodes; as long as I have strength and life I will never abandon you."

He hugged me and said: "I will not thank you for I am sure of your heart," then, putting a finger to his lips: "Say nothing, my brother, of this to anyone for it would not be understood by the regiment whom I am leaving. Remove your uniform and dress plainly. When it gets light, we will leave Częstochowa quietly." Hearing this I could not sleep, though I had felt the need for it, and started to get ready for travel. I wrapped my leather money-belt around myself, noting that it contained over 100 gold ducats some of which I had from home, others that I took from Cossack saddlebags which were never empty. I put on plain trousers and a dark blue jacket without any decorations and put two pistols in my holsters. Pulaski was not sleeping, he was busy writing a farewell letter to the regiment which he did in a fine and sincere style so that (as we later learned) everyone, even the toughest soldiers, wept while listening to it being read. I saved a copy of this letter and would have quoted it here but I lost it together with some baggage during our unhappy adventures in Turkey (of which I will write later).

24.   I had a great desire to say goodbye to my good friend and relative Kalasanty Bzowski, but then I would have to reveal the secret, so with pain in my heart I decided not to. I knelt before my pictured of the Blessed Virgin (which hung above my bed) and prayed with ardor to that Queen of Poland, begging her to protect our unhappy nation and placing myself and Pulaski under her protection, asking her to guard and protect us among the many hazards which we were about to face. I barely finished my prayer when Bohdanek, Pulaski's cossack (who accompanied him from childhood and whom he liked tremendously) came and reported quietly that all were asleep in the fortress and that the horses were saddled and ready for travel. I took the pistols under my arm and went to the second courtyard following the wall, for it was still night, dark and cloudy. In a few minutes Pulaski was there; we mounted and each of us, after making the sign of the cross, started in great silence through a side entrance of the fortress. Once we traveled a distance, Pulaski who had remained silent, stopped his horse and spoke to me pointing with his hand toward Częstochowa. "Had this not been a holy

place and had there not been so many mementos dear to Polish history, I would not let it go, my brother, but would have defended it to the last and been buried in its rubble. I know the men would have been with me, but Radziminski was right. I need no holy grave, this Palladium of the Rzeczpospolita [Polish Republic] may not be given to the anti-papists [Protestants] for their despoiling."

Pulaski at the walls of Jasna Góra Monastery in 1770, by Juliusz Kossak

Book Six

Travel through Silesia, Saxony, Bavaria, etc. - Meeting the Princess of Courland in Dresden - the Generality in Braunau - Mazowiecki in Turkey

1.   Pulaski's first intent was to make his way to Turkey as the only country in Europe that had made a sincere declaration to support the Confederation and helped it more than the Court of Versailles, taking up war against Russia. But there were great difficulties in making one's way across such a stretch of country that had various armies about. What is more important, the Divan [Turkish Court] was weakening and entering into negotiations with Russia, sending its plenipotentiary to Bucharest for discussions. It was not wise then to get into Turkish clutches and take risks without any advantage for our public cause, and make such a long and hazardous journey. The Prussian border was nearby and in Silesian cities were many of our citizens who were too cowardly to fight and sought safety outside our borders. There were few Prussian army units there because the bulk of them had moved toward Torun. Farther on in Dresden were many Polish malcontents who were part of the Prince of Courland's retinue. For these reasons and others we steered toward Prussia.

2.   In Opole (or Oppolen in German) we met a nobleman from Kalisz, whose name today I can't remember. He was an incredible braggart and liar. He told us of his many successes and wartime deeds while under Malczewski's command. He counted fifty Russians whom he killed with his own hand and there were other tall tales in which there was not one word of truth. This was a nobleman who was an obvious coward; who definitely did not care for the smell of gunpowder; and for this reason decided to hide his cowardice in Silesia. But he tripped up most severely when he said that he knew Casimir Pulaski well, having served under him in the expedition to Lithuania. Pulaski had a good laugh listening to the boastful stories told by this braggart but did not contravene him, for there was no point. Moreover, this noble from Kalisz was an entertaining and useful man. When we told him that we were escaping, the Krakow Confederacy having been crushed, and were proceeding to

Dresden and to join Prince Charles [Karol of Courland], he made our passage easier by showing us the way and providing a letter to a German friend in Swidnica. He was the first to tell us the news about the coming partition planned by Russia, Prussia and Austria. At first we could not believe this, thinking that this was another fabrication of his, but unfortunately (as it later turned out) it was the pure truth!

3.　　　While we traveled I used my own name while Pulaski identified himself as Jan Karczewski, whereupon the Kalisz noble stated that the Karczewskis were his cousins, by way of his mother. Pulaski had a full money belt and paid for everything, not letting me spend a penny. But when I told him of my money supply he said, "Keep it hidden for when times get bad, I still have some cash and will not let you pay for my expenses." Bohdanek was a faithful and cheerful companion, always sober, always alert, looking after our horses and baggage as if these were his eye teeth. Sometimes to cheer us he would sing the sad Ukrainian tunes, so that on hearing a few notes we nearly cried a tear. Our conversations were not especially happy, not uncommon among exiles who were leaving their beloved homeland for God knows how long. And the times for the homeland were going to be bad, and to soothe us there was only a bit of hope in the righteousness of our holy cause and God's providence!

4.　　　After five days of travel we reached Swidnica which the Germans call Szweydne in their language. The letter written by the Kalisz noble was very helpful, because in the villages the folk speak Polish, but in the cities all is German including the language which we didn't speak. Pulaski knew French and I knew Latin, as much as the Jesuit Fathers had taught me, but in Silesia these two tongues were of no use. Fortunately our German host, a decent human being, spoke Polish well for he was once a practical medic for Lubomirski, starosta of Kazimierz [town] and after his employer died our German returned to his hometown to practice medicine. Here I will say in parenthesis that in those times there were no native doctors in Poland, only Germans or Jews, for local Poles, especially the nobles with crests, had an aversion to this profession; considering work done with a syringe or a lancet below their honor. They did blood-letting only with a sabre, taking it from the trunk or the head — from their own countrymen at the local political meetings or from the enemies of the Rzeczpospolita [Poland] on the battlefield. Thus this German took good care of us for two days, having learned hospitality in Poland — from where he brought back quite a sum of money for his rhubarb and other Latin prescriptions. He told us how to reach Dresden, taking the road through Zittawa and Gorzelice, which the latter the Germans call Gorlitz.

5.   We made our way to Dresden for there resided the Prince of Courland and his wife, daughter of Krasinski, starosta of Nowomiejsk, whom the prince — son of the dear departed king — did marry in secret during his father's lifetime in Warsaw; and now after his death took to Dresden with him. Pulaski as a sixteen-year-old boy spent time in Starosta Krasinski's house and did fall in love with the one who later became the princess. It is said that she displayed affection toward him, but later when the Lubomirskis brought her to Warsaw and Prince Charles made his sincere sentiments known, young Franciszka — impressed with the rank of a pretender to the throne — forgot about Casimir, the Starosta of Warka. But Pulaski did not forget her, though as a good Catholic and an honest cavalier — seeing that the sacrament of marriage had separated him forever from his love — wanted to maintain for her a loyal heart and a pure friendship. He was not the author of the idea, but he did support those who favored Prince Charles during the Bar Confederation for the Polish throne, consoling himself that his Franciszka will put on the crown and he would make the way to the throne possible for her. We also knew that Rostworowski, starosta of Zytomierz, was in Dresden on Confederation business at the Saxon court and that Lady Moszynska, friend of the Courland princess, a good and respected woman known to Pulaski and me, was there as well. We hoped that these persons would tell us what happened to the Generality when it was chased out of Preszow and where we must go to effectively help our homeland.

6.   On 8th of July we entered Dresden, the Saxon capital, an orderly city beautifully built, with wondrous palaces and churches of the finest construction. Rostworowski had already left, but Lady Moszynska greeted us courteously as a true friend. She informed us that Krasinski, Pac, Oginski, and Bohusz, not knowing where to run, hid for a time in Vienna in the apartment of the ambassador serving the French Cardinal de Rohan. This Monsignor got them papers for travel through the Austrian lands to Bavaria - in which direction they departed meaning to stop at Munich (or Mnichow as we call it). She advised us that we should wait in Dresden to see which way the wind would blow, bringing perhaps some intervention in our plight from either France or Turkey. It was good advice, so we stayed with her, especially that we were most

Carl Christian Joseph of Saxony (1733 - 1796) by Pietro Rotari, 1755

Franciszka Krasinski by Krafft the Elder, 1768

weary from the journey and our anxious hearts needed some kind of solace.

7.   A few days later, kind Lady Moszynska took Pulaski in her carriage to see the Princess of Courland who did not live at the Elector's palace — as she by law deserved — but at a separate manor on the outskirts of Dresden. Though her marriage to the Prince was publicly announced, the Saxon court did not want give her the title or rank of princess. How the meeting between the two lovers went after thirteen years of separation, I can't say for I was not an eyewitness. Because of discretion, I did not ask for details, but after a few hours Pulaski returned depressed and sad. He said that he had seen the Princess and that they spoke long and with affection for the Confederation, he added with a sigh: "Maciej! The purple [royalty] and honors give no contentment and poor Franciszka is most unhappy." Later, I somehow learned that Prince Charles' old love for his wife had cooled and he neglected her, chasing after other women; though the princess was still young having but thirty years and being uncommonly beautiful.

8.   In Dresden there were many Poles some of whom supported the Saxon court, and the others were travelers who had sought to find a safe haven during the troubles in their homeland. All would come to Lady Moszynska's or to the Mniewski home, greeting each other in person, but telling bad things about each other in private. Everyone had a point of view and it happened that one Lisiecki started saying to others that Casimir Pulaski was bribed by Salder with the sum of two-thousand red zlotys to leave the Confederation. There is in our nation such a flaw that through envy or vanity they like to make foul gossip about persons who have done service to the homeland. This is not the only example. When in the times of king Jan Kazimierz Stefan Czarniecki chased the Swedes out of the country and saved the Rzeczpospolita; some of the magnates looked at him cross-eyed and said *how was it possible for such a petty noble to possibly deserve a seat in the Senate* while sowing various lies about him. And what about Smigielski, of honorable memory, who during the time of Augustus II, beat the Saxon army — was he not accused of being a traitor? Not so long ago, [Jozef] Pulaski Starosta of Warka, a gray-haired old man, like old Priam of Troy, sacrificed himself and his sons in the service of his homeland; and did he not run afoul of the intrigues the Potockis hatched, and was he not put under arrest where from worry and grief did he not suffer the end of his virtuous life? Should it then be that his son, the great cavalier and worthy warrior of

Poland, would not escape the evil of human tongues! After all these years my heart breaks when I write of this great injustice. Our Lord Christ said that Jerusalem murdered its prophets; so our Rzeczpospolita should weep that we do stone our finest sons. Forgive them Lord, for they do not know what they do!

9.   I did not know about these calumnies but Lisiecki was so persistent in spreading these lies that they got back to Pulaski who immediately challenged him to a duel and so did he punish this villain that he had to take back all his foul accusations and then sneak out of Dresden where everyone tormented him by repeating insulting jokes about the duel. The thing went like this. They dueled with swords and we know that Pulaski was a master in fencing, so had he wanted he could have split Lisiecki's skull but merely contented himself with carving off his right ear. Thus, Lisiecki, by losing an ear came out (so they said) shamefully and attracted the laughter of the populace for it was repeated that he whose tongue wags too much shall be shorn of an ear. This and other remarks caused him to flee and so there was peace among us for a time. Even though all respected Pulaski and no one believed these accusations, they were repeated thoughtlessly, so had not Pulaski punished Lisiecki there might have been a few simple minded sops who would have believed the rumor. But the amputated ear put a stop to all of this. Pulaski, however, was most affected, for he was a fiery man and felt it all deeply, especially the injustice of it. Sometimes when mentioning it he had tears in his eyes, and it took all of my persuasions, the goodness of Lady Moszynska and the good advice of the Prince of Courland to calm him down.

10.   There took place in Dresden another duel caused by a pun, and this is how it happened. A few of us went to the Hungarian [tavern?] to empty a few bottles of wine, not to get drunk but to take on a better humor. In the discussion it came up that Lithuanian surnames are usually short; for example: Pac, Los, Karp etc. While those in the [Polish] Kingdom are long and end in ski. Two different peoples, to be sure, but Kulinski, a ready wit, said: "So that if a person of the Kingdom had the name Kiepski [the pun is that the word "kiepski" means "shoddy"] — and if he lost the ski he would become a Lithuanian!" All roared with laughter, except for one, because in the company we had but one Lithuanian, and he had a short name, that being Szczyt. This man was offended by such characterization of Lithuanians and challenged Kulinski to a duel. They used pistols and shot twice, both times without effect,

even though the second time they stood six paces apart. After that their seconds and other Poles were able to settle the matter, stating correctly, that the matter was a jest while drinking, and it was not worth to have two such fine cavaliers kill each other just to prove their manhood and determination. They shook hands and went off happily.

11.   The important political happenings then taking place took our attention away from these trifles. The partition of the Rzeczpospolita by three powers was no longer a secret. Sir von Effen, the Saxon representative in Warsaw, had sent news of it to the Court and all of Germany was buzzing with the news. We were most unhappy about the coming of this great storm cloud, hoping that the rain which may fall would be gentle. Meanwhile, we got thunder and lightning aimed with great power at our unhappy country. So it is that speculations are mainly in error and Almighty God often punishes the innocent for the sins of their fathers. May His holy will be blessed! In that time our commanders who were the Generality, had settled in Bavaria and wrote a protest, that came from Bohusz's pen, sending it to the Sultan in Stanbul and to the Dutch newspapers.

12.   I once went with Pulaski to dinner with the Princess of Courland. She lived in her manor but not in a showy way — enough for the daughter of a Polish magnate but not enough for the wife of a prince. Here was a lady of rare wisdom and virtuous sentiments, and uncommonly beautiful. Her body was lean, her face smooth but pale — possibly from worry. Her eyes were lively and engaging, with a voice that was most pleasant and captivated the soul. Pulaski, a man of courage and solid constitution, trembled in her presence as if standing before the Father Rector [at school ?]. I did pity him for I knew that it was concealed sentiment which brought on this timidity. We spoke much about this and that, but mostly about the situation in the Rzeczpospolita. The princess knew well about the wartime deeds of Pulaski and heaped upon him well-deserved praises and urged him to endure. She mentioned that Prince Charles was truly loyal to Poland, which was not his second, but his first homeland. There were other discussions of former times when the princess was but a simple Starosta's daughter and spent time with Pulaski. Knowing their secret I looked at her carefully and noticed that, while speaking of this, her cheek reddened, but Pulaski also blushed. But both maintained proper manners as required of a virtuous lady and a true cavalier who were separated by the sacrament of marriage!

13.   We had already spent a few months in Dresden when a new companion arrived, Captain Wielichowski; who had grown very much attached to Pulaski. He told us that he was an eyewitness when, a few days after our departure, Suvarov and a large army came to Często-chowa demanding its surrender. Radziminski answered he would only surrender to the Polish king, and would only give the Jasna Gora into the charge of the royal forces. So the Russians stormed the walls several times but were always repelled suffering losses. Finally, on August 15th there came orders from Warsaw that the fortress should be surrendered. So Radziminski, with pain in his heart, obeyed the king's order. The Russians did not harm the defenders (as they did when taking the Krakow fortress, that I already mentioned). All were allowed to go freely. Suvarov, though of the Orthodox Church, made an example of praying before the altar of the Sacred Virgin and did not let anyone harm the monks. In this way he showed himself better than the Protestant Drewicz who threw blasphemies at the Mother of God, and for this he did suffer punishment at our sinful hands.

14.   Not much later, Pulaski received letters from the Generality bidding him come to the city of Braunau in Bavaria where Krasinski, Pac and others who left Munich were staying. He was asked to attend a council on the fate of the endangered Rzeczpospolita. To this call he could not shut his ears, but hurried there forthwith. Though Dresden was a paradise to us, we went on our way bidding farewells to Prince Charles and the Princes, and Lady Moszynska who was like a mother to us. Likewise, with the other Poles who poured blessings upon us, wishing us a safe journey an a rapid return. The trip went well but the return never took place for God had other things in mind! We had come to Dresden rather unhappy, and now we left with our hearts even sadder, for we were leaving behind a whole group of dear friends and going out into the world, farther and farther from our beloved homeland.

15.   The details of our journey are not worth writing down, for what is there to say? Our coach turned over once, but God preserved us from harm. During our overnight stay in Pilzen, Bohdanek beat up four Czechs — and there were similar insignificant incidents. I'd prefer to get down to brass tacks and give a picture of our Generality which we found in Braunau. The chief persona were: Michal Krasinski, the blood brother of the Kamieniec Bishop, the Royal Marshal; General Michal Pac, Marshal General of Lithuania; and Ignacy Bohusz, secretary of the Confederation. All three well fattened, of short stature but combative,

especially Krasinski and Bohusz. The first was friendly, humorous and a reveler; the other full of information and very eloquent. Both were men of energy, of such there are few; and dressed in the Polish fashion. Michal Pac had a plain face, but was educated, and his manner was so courteous and sweet that he would be a balm to place on a wound. Pac dressed in French clothes with a whig and short jacket and with his gentle manner mitigated his two more pugnacious companions. Oginski had already departed for London, but we met there two other gentlemen, Wiesolowski and Lninski.

16.   Each of these men had a fair supply of money, in addition to which the Vienna based banker Brear, sent them the remaining amount from the French subsidies deposited with him. Thus they could live in a grand style, in the noble manner, giving receptions and parties. Just as locust will go into an open beehive, all the Poles from various places in the German Reich came to dine at their tables in Braunau. There were many there and among them some persons not known to anyone, hangers-on, idlers and fops worth nothing and of bad character. I will give one sad example here. Shortly after our arrival in Braunau the decent and worthy Mr. Lninski died and was laid out in his home on a catafalque dressed quite properly. On the day of the funeral we came to the house and saw that the crucifix he had in his folded hands, as was proper for a Catholic burial, had been removed and a Jack of Clubs inserted in its place. One of the young idlers made an improper jest because the dead man had been an inveterate card player. We were most offended by the sacrilege. I don't know which one did it but I'm sure that God had punished him — for a dead body is a holy thing, even for the Protestants and the Moslems.

17.   We spent several months in Braunau. Pulaski went to the councils but there was no agreement. The two impulsive men, Krasinski and Bohusza, were now joined by Pulaski, who was also quick to action and an outspoken fellow besides. It was no use for Pac to try to calm them; the Generality was boiling over like a pot of overheated water. Bohusz respected Pulaski and even loved him, but the two magnates could not forget that at one time the elder Pulaski represented the Czartoryskis in court. So many times they let Pulaski know their displeasure — not openly but in devious ways, because he would not let himself be teased — but in a noble and courtly manner. Tired of this and seeing that his presence there would do no good, Pulaski decided to leave Braunau (especially since he was not a member of the Generality, but was only

called to consult).

18.　　We left in the middle of January in the year of Our Lord 1773 for Frankfurt where Karp and Wielichowski were staying and after crossing much of the German country, we stopped. There we learned that a Manifesto had been published by the Three Powers about the partitions. Russia released our senators who were kept in Kaluga, and that an extraordinary Sejm [Congress of the Polish Nobility] was convened for April 19th. Each day brought worse news. The Sejm had transformed itself into a confederation under the command of Poninski, a man of poor reputation a sycophant of the king and a Russian sympathizer; thus he had the support of Sztakelberg. The deputies from Nowogrod, the well remembered Tadeusz Reytan and Samuel Korsak, protested bravely and eloquently, opposing this violence like Cato the Roman did of old. But when the armies of the Three Powers entered Warsaw and surrounded the place where the deputies met — Poniatowski became frightened and wept (the only real talent he had was in being able to cry — a virtue in a beaver, but not in a king) begging the Sejm not to worsen the situation with useless opposition. Then a delegation was chosen which later shamefully approved the action of the Tree Powers.

19.　　Each day brought new alarms. Every newspaper, every letter reported new disasters and unhappiness. Only one letter contained hope. It was from Mazowiecki, Commander of the Confederation in the Dobrzyn lands, a good man and a determined cavalier. After the Bar Confederation was scattered Mazowiecki and several officers made it to Turkey and while staying in Sylistrya with his men, learned from a French traveler who happened by, that the Generality and Pulaski were in Braunau in Bavaria, so at the next opportunity he expedited a letter which Bohusz then forwarded to Frankfurt. In the letter Mazowiecki stated that the Turks will be making war on Russia; and the Poles are being treated fairly and there is the promise of protection and care from the excesses of the Three Powers. Already some of our Confederates gathered around him (some were in Turkey since 1768) waiting to take up arms against our common foe alongside the Ottoman army. He invited Pulaski to come and lose no more time among the Germans, but hurry to Sylistrya and take over command of the Poles who await his coming like rain in the desert. Pulaski and all of us were glad to hear this news and grabbed onto this hope which was as a gossamer spider web that could easily break and make all our efforts useless and only cause more misery (about this later).

20.   On the same day as we received Mazowiecki's letter there arrived at our place a strange man who was telling incredible and miraculous things. He was a Pole, but would not tell us his family name. He was dressed like a priest in a broad hat, in a long black robe much like that the Jews wear, and was wrapped about the middle with a rope like a monk. He said that he had a vision of St. Stanislaw Bishop and Martyr, protector of the Rzeczpospolita, who told him to preach to the Poles that the Three Partitioning Powers, soon will be punished. That St. Petersburg will be subject to destruction by water, Vienna by the air [plague], and Berlin by fire. Poland would be ruled by a king born on an island with great power and have extensive borders, etc. He spoke easily and with force while in his eyes was something frightening and it seemed he was a madman. But when Pulaski made an accurate observation that since the prophet had a mission from St. Stanislaw then he should preach his message in Poland not in the German lands; the man replied (lifting up his finger heavenward) that such was the will of God and there the star leads him. This strange man spent a day in Frankfurt and then went to some unknown locality. The money we offered him to pay his way he refused, but only partook of food and rest with us. Then we heard no more of him. No doubt he was caught and put into the loony-bin, for his speech and behavior certainly qualified him for it.

21.   At about this time we learned from the newspapers that the investigation into the king's abduction had been concluded. Lukaski and Cybulski were beheaded in Warsaw and Pulaski, though absent (and on whom the entire blame was placed) was also condemned to death. This unjust verdict did sadden Pulaski and he wrote a protest against this verdict, which in its first version was clear and honest. But unfortunately, Karp through overzealousness and bad advice persuaded him to deny any participation in this unfortunate affair. Despite my advice, the Marshal let himself be turned, and wrote a second version according to Karp's suggestion, sending it to e Dutch newspaper where I read it as printed (for having nothing to do I decided to study French and was pretty good at it). In time Pulaski regretted it but it was too late, for it was already on the printed page, and it did not change public opinion at all.

22.   As we know, Pulaski was not the author of the plot to abduct the king, but when Strawinski told him of this plan, he did not object and even promised his aid. On the designated day he took a troop of men toward Warsaw where the conspirators were to meet. But there

was no intent to murder the king, the best proof being what Pulaski said to Radziminski in my presence after the plot failed: "I'm glad that is happened this way, Sir, because what would I do with this *Ciolek* [ciolek = calf] (for this was the Poniatowski crest)." When Radziminski replied "Had they killed him, it would have been no great loss, for any other successor would have been better. And if Russia put Repnin on the throne of the Rzeczpospolita, he might have been better than this greedy incompetent." On hearing this Pulaski barked at him: "I could agree to dethronement but never to murder! Let the English kill their kings, but Polish and Catholic hands have not and never will be stained with such blood." Then he added that he would have received the king in Często-chowa with proper respect and through persuasion he could lead him to see a better way, avoiding any violence. Those who accuse Pulaski of regicide, should see if those would be words spoken by a murderer.

23.   Meanwhile, war broke out in Turkey. When the negotiations in Bucharest broke, down Rumiancow crossed the Danube at the head of the Russian army at the beginning of June and went against a large and strong Turkish army, led by the blundering Vizier Muzum-Oglu. So at the beginning the Russians had the better of it, they beat the Turks twice, but when they reached Sylistrya and started a siege on the city they found it a nut too hard to crack. The garrison commander was a man of great heart and military talent. Meanwhile, Mazowiecki and his con-federates did not just sit there like a bunch of painted beauties, but built up the Turks by giving them plenty of examples in courage. Many raids were made out of the city, so that the Russian army recently enjoying easy success and became dispirited — having to take the city and get-ting beaten repeatedly — ceased the siege retreating toward the Danube. During this unhappy retreat General Weymarn's corps was totally scat-tered, and the commander fell on the field of battle. Had the Turks been able to take advantage of these victories, probably not one live Russian would have escaped. These news reached us in Frankfurt and encour-aged our rapidly beating hearts. We started to make serious preparations to go to Turkey.

24.   Our Generality moved from Braunau to Augusburg, and from there to the free city of Lindau, sending from there two well written and strongly argued petitions authored by Bohusz to the Sultan in Stanbul, and also had them printed in the papers. Pulaski being in communication with Bohusz and the Princess of Courland told them about his intent of

going to Turkey, and this idea was praised in Lindau and Dresden. The kind princess, though not rich and having no obligations toward us, sent to us via banker Kuntz, a thousand red zlotys to pay for the costs of the journey. These funds came as if from heaven, and were most useful as Pulaski (who paid for everything) was beginning to run short of cash. Karp, who was of ill health but had a chest full of Lithuanian thallers (which he tried to conceal but we well knew) stayed in Germany. Meanwhile, Pulaski, Wielichowski and I, with our faithful Bohdanek, placing ourselves under the Almighty's protection, left Frankfurt to meet new and unexpected dangers (about which I will write in the next book).

Book Seven

Arrival in Turkey - At the Camp of the Grand Vizier at Szumla - Scattering of the Turkish Army - Stay at Adrianopol and Rodosto

1.　　We left Frankfurt at the end of December and did not arrive in Sylistrya until March 10th in the Year of Our Lord 1774 on the day of the Forty Holy Martyrs, which was also a prophecy of our future fate; for it seemed that we were but a handful of Christians tossed out to be martyred among the Muslims. If I had wanted to write out all the details of our long journey, partly by ship but mostly by land on horseback and in carriages, I would run out of vellum. For we saw many interesting things, foreign countries and cities aplenty. The people we met - Germans, Swiss, Italians, Venetians, Dalmatians, Bosnians, Serbs, Bulgars and others. But since I decided that in these books I would write only about political incidents connected to our country, thus I will not mention these things which are more suitable to and better left for geographers and scientists than to me, a soldier. I would like to add in parenthesis that the city I liked best was Venice where we spent about a week resting.

2.　　Venice is called *beautiful* by its inhabitants and rightly so. It is built on water, probably on oaken pilings and has palaces and churches so richly and finely built that there are none like them in Warsaw or Krakow. Never did I see any like them in the German states. In addition to a market ringed with shapely buildings, there is no place to walk, save the bridges. Even the oldest of the inhabitants cannot remember that there was ever in Venice a carriage or a horse while for getting around; they use long black painted boats covered with a canopy that are called *gondolas*. The people are very busy and the women are unusually beautiful, having great affection for foreigners. We visited the churches of which the choicest was that of St. Mark, patron saint of Venice; and also the state arsenal which was arranged for us by the French representative as the local government is very suspicious and often does not want foreigners looking at their secrets and sources of power.

3.   Mazowiecki and other Confederates staying in Sylistrya received us with open arms, crying with joy. On the next day Pulaski went to see the Pasha who was commander of the garrison (for Sylistrya is a strong fortress). The interpreter was a certain Suski, a Mazurian living in Turkey who left Bar in 1768 and wandered around, eventually becoming a Moslem (which he denied before us, making the sign of the cross and repeating the cardinal articles of faith). The Pasha knew about Pulaski, me, and Wielichowski (that we were all noblemen and *Effendi* [lords], as the Turks say) and he received us most sincerely, speaking of this and that; about the unjust occupation of our country, about the Generality, about Poniatowski, the Russian army, about Rumiancow etc.; all with great intelligence and propriety. He had us come and light up gilded pipes filled with a strange tobacco and to drink he offered us coffee in small cups which the Turks savor greatly. We Poles would have preferred Hungarian wine over this, or even some old mead. When we left, he sent to our house four fine horses with complete equipment for war. This was a great boon for aside from pistols we had no weapons.

4.   Pulaski took command over the Confederate forces, only forty in number but consisting of determined and brave men. (We had hoped that this regiment would grow, because in Poland there were news of it and many volunteers were making their way to join us.) All went along a military schedule with Pulaski exercising the troops in the German manner which he liked and wanted us to learn. But when Sulmirski, a fearsome fighter and a rider of the old school, started to mutter under his nose about what use these German maneuvers were going to do us when we had good old Polish *fencing techniques* and *accuracy in firing pistols*. Hearing this muttering Pulaski shouted at him saying: "This fencing of yours was good in the past but now our enemies have gotten ahead of us, so we must learn their secrets to defeat them in the field. Whether good or bad, it is my will. I have no intention of being a figurehead, and since I have command you must listen to me." Hearing this Sulmirski reflected on his words and shut-up asking the marshal's forgiveness and exercised the German maneuvers with us; forming up by threes and other new practices.

5.   So with God's grace and in good health we spent our time well occupied. Once in a while there was a bit of drinking or feasting but only to cheer us up and put us in a good mood, as we would not offend God with dissipation. Saddest of all was that in the Turkish city there was no church or Catholic priest, so we could not go and hear Holy

Venice in the 1770's by Canaletto

Topkai Palace in Constantinople

Mass. So we adopted the following manner. We gathered in a large hall and had Sulmirski, the eldest, read from a *mass book* the prayers that were used at service, and then the litanies and antiphonies, to which we answered as was necessary. Thus doing, we served God and our homeland — praying first and then preparing for war, ready to spill our sinful blood; for which the occasion came, and this I will soon relate.

6.　　The Russian army received significant reinforcements in men (who for greater speed were transported in wagons to the borders of the [Russian] Empire and to Wolyn and started to move forward. Marshal Rumiancow and his Generals Ungern, Potemkin and Dolhoruki organized their army and led it across the Danube above Sylistrya, near a large lake. Pulaski advised the Pasha that we should deny them passage; and this would have been an easy thing to do, causing confusion and damage to the Russians. But the Pasha had faith in his *Allah* — what the Turks call God — and said: "That which is to happen, will be. If Allah wishes it, the Russians will drown, if not they will come here." There was no argument against this Moslem theology. Allah did not deign to drown the enemy, and they crossed with their feet dry and without any trouble. Soon Ungern's corps came to attack Sylistrya, but he had no luck with it, for the Turks fought him from the walls and by sending out sorties. In these our regiment performed excellently, fighting like noblemen. We did lose one of our men, Jan Ruszkowski, who was hit in the heart with a bullet and Wielichowski was cut on his arm but not seriously. So Ungern ceased the siege, and Pulaski took advantage of it (with the Pasha's permission) taking us out of the fortress into the field, toward where the Grand Vizier's army was camped with all its baggage trains near Szumla, where we could be of better use. After a few days march we successfully reached them.

7.　　Pulaski had written documents from the Pasha in Sylistrya to the Grand Vizier which gave him ready access to this Turkish commander. Muzum-Oglu received us sincerely and with honors, having tents given to us and indicating our position in the camp. But at this first conference Pulaski saw that things will be taking a bad turn, because the Vizier was a soft and effeminate man, without any toughness or determination. Returning from the meeting he said to me: "There will be no bread from this flour; these Turks are good for nothing, their blood has thickened in their veins, they are fat and sleepy. The Russians will wake them up, but by then it will be too late." We looked with admiration at the magnificence of the camp, the fabulous horses, cannon and other military trappings. The tents of the Pashas and Colonels (whom they call *Czobardis*) shone from the silk and gold thread; and the men were numerous like ants, all the biggest men, choice soldiers, but for all that they had such a weak commander. Here Pulaski found Osman Aga, leader of the janissaries whom he knew well in Chocim during his first stay in Turkey after Bar fell. Osama was a friendly man of good will and of true noble character. Great service he did for our regiment in obtaining food for our men and horses. He rendered even greater service on another sad occasion (which I will relate below).

8.   While the Turks just sat there inactive, as if in the garden of Allah, Rumiancow deployed his corps and approached quietly in an enveloping movement. It happened that the Vizier's army was cut off from its supplies. Soltykow at the head of a few thousand men moved to the side and surprised a strongly armed Turkish convoy bringing food to the camp. There were thirty thousand Turkish troops whom he totally scattered, part of them laid dead in the field. He captured several thousand wagons of flour, biscuits and other provisions, taking some away and burning the rest. It is hard to imagine the fear that arose in the Muslim camp when they heard the sad news, even more when they saw Rumiancow right before them. There was a chance to save them from hunger and final destruction, taking on a general battle and winning (which could have happened). But the Turks, once their foot slips, loose their heads and despair and then go down to their own destruction without any resistance.

9.   So it happened. It is hard to tell it in words or understand, if you were not an eye witness. Perhaps it will be like this on the terrible day of the Last Judgment and Resurrection, something my sinful eyes have not seen before. For there was such confusion and such terrible screaming and lament that the human ear has not ever heard, except perhaps on the day of the Great Flood or when fire fell upon Sodom. Pulaski and I mounted and went to skirmish with the forward guard of the Russian army. One of their officers recognized us and shouted: "Sobaki (Lachy) [that is Poles] as Mazowiecki was at him and sliced his head with a sabre whereupon the officer cursed and dropped dead on the ground giving up his unclean spirit. This was the one success of Polish arms, for not seeing any reinforcements and the enemy forces coming in strength, we had to retreat to the camp from whence came sporadic cannon fire. But even that stopped as we passed the outpost and found the entire camp in great disorder. All were fleeing in chaos,

leaving the cannon and tents — throwing away their weapons. Pulaski broke through to the Grand Vizier's tent asking for orders as what to do, but the incompetent Muzum-Oglu, already on horseback, told him: "I have no particular orders for you, do as you see others do." Meanwhile, the others were fleeing in desperation so, with pain in our hearts, we did — as they say — *skedaddle*. Getting into company with crows one must crow; and with Turks one must run, though in the past it was not so!

10.   The huge Turkish army left the place of battle hardly firing a shot or offering resistance and fell apart. Rumiancow had an easy victory, seized rich booty, spilling a lot of Muslim blood without any damage to himself. A few miles from the camp they stopped the chase but the Turks kept running, still frightened. This was done in no military order but in groups, and all shouting, both those mounted and on foot, to Allah for succor and lamenting to high heaven. Our regiment moved in order without any great hurry, while those who fled passed us and shook their fists at us, saying something in Turkish. Those who understood translated that: it was we who caused the defeat for Allah and his prophet has punished them for associating with Christians. In vain we shouted at them: *Dost* and *Kardasz*, that is "friends, brothers!" They comprehended nothing, throwing accusations at us. So unenlightened is this nation that is has no understanding; like cattle with human faces.

11.   It was well into the evening when we reached the bank of a small river where we intended to make our camp for the night. At this time a group of mounted Turks came toward us — about fifty men of their cavalry. As they reached us they shouted threats, one being the loudest, yelling: *Issewa hazyr* at the top of his lungs. I asked Suski what was meant and he says: "the man is calling you a Christian swine." Oh, wait you pagan! (I thought). And when he continued his insults I was seized by impatience, my right palm itching something awful, I grabbed my saber and had at him. The Turk raised his weapon and we exchanged strokes. Then I struck him with great force, his head went down and he fell from the saddle. Unfortunately, my impetuosity drew some unhappy consequences. The Turks, on seeing their companion slain, went at the Poles and we had an intense fight. I thought: "Now that I've brewed some bitter beer, at least I should have a drink" and went at them. The fight lasted about half-hour. Six of our men fell, among them Sulmirski, but there were twenty dead Turks without counting the wounded, and they withdrew. Then a new regiment came up, they took heart and were

at us again. It was getting plenty hot, for now they had a swarm of about two-hundred while there were but thirty of us Poles. Fortunately, God's providence was with us for the commander of this new regiment was Osman Aga, Pulaski's friend who recognized us and stopped his men. When our interpreter explained things, how we were abused with insults and had to defend ourselves for no reason, the matter was settled! But this did not return life to our dear departed. We buried them decently, though without church ceremonies and in unhallowed ground.

12.　　And in this way I caused the deaths of these people. Pulaski gave me real chiding and many a time I begged God for forgiveness and may He let it pass. For any nobleman and cavalry man worthy his crest being in my place, would have done the same — to protect his honorable Christian name good and proper, and punish the barking of a Muslim dog. As for the rest, like it or not, as Wielichowski said "what is done cannot be undone." And a God who saved me from this fray (where I was quite active and risked by neck) knew my innocence for I was saved from death, and never got even a scratch from it! May His Holy name be blessed!"

13.　　This sudden retreat by the Turkish forces put paid to any ideas that the Turks could beat the Russians which would benefit our homeland. It also caused us personal loss and depression. During the general alarm in camp all of us mounted and then during the confusion and retreat there was no time to go back to the tents and pack the wagons. Thus we lost all our baggage, and whatever clothes and possessions we had. We were (as the saying goes) as naked as a Turkish saint. Pulaski left all his money in the tent and probably Rumiancow's cossacks took it, together with our dear Bohdanek who was guarding it. It turned out that from all our wealth, only my money belt was left, which I wore twisted about me like a snake. For several days we rode very hungry, but not cold, through some great mountains and empty valleys, tired, plagued by want, and sunk into dark thoughts. It was the faithful Osman Aga (who saved us from the recent troubles) who accompanied us with his men and tried to console us with his Muslim theology — that all this was Allah's will.

14.　　On the fifth day sorely tired and half dead with hunger we came to Adrianopol, a great Turkish city, situated among green gardens, which was a welcome sight after the Balkan deserts. Many Christians live in this city, mostly French and Venetian merchants who, on learning that a group of Poles racked with want and unhappiness has arrived, gathered about us not too see an unhappy sight, but like brothers in Christ, to give a helping hand. They did as the Holy Writ commanded, feeding the hungry and giving drink to the thirsty. They divided us among themselves, as they were able, taking us into their homes to give us great affection and to aid us in our sufferings. The Turks are merciful even to animals (one must give them that) but such a sincere welcome could have only been given to us by Christians.

15.   Pulaski and I were quartered with a wealthy French man named Arnoux who conducted a great trade in wheat and had his storehouses and offices in Stanbul. Our host was glad to find that Pulaski spoke his language well, while I managed only so-so, but still had to recount the details of our miserable journey and unfortunate adventures. Here I must add in parenthesis that the French are very curious and talkative people — but have great affection for our country, especially since the time that their [Prince Henri] Valois came to the Rzeczpospolita on invitation to take the Polish throne, though we know he did not long stay there. But that was not our fault! Mr. Arnoux took good care of us, in a noble way as it seemed (him being a merchant) though not having a crest. But in France people of all stations and rank are wont to act out of noble sentiment. His wife, a serious matronly woman, was most courteous to us, while his most uncommonly pretty daughters took to us like two domesticated kittens, giggling and singing various French airs with us to the accompaniment of a guitar. In a word, since Dresden, we never had it so good.

16.   Our Confederation companions also had it good in their lodgings; all had comforts aplenty. Those that knew Latin (and more than half did) had the better of it for by this means they could communicate with the French and Venetians easier than by using Polish. This cheered us in our sad situation, but the greatest joy was the return of Bohdanek whom we thought lost forever. This faithful servant, seeing what was going on, with the whole camp panicked and fleeing, packed all of his master's things, placed them on a horse and sought to find us in the crowd, but to no avail. So he went ahead and for ten days wandered among the scattered army, not knowing the language, and with no bread to eat. Feeding only on unripe fruit, at last he reached Adrianopol. Turkish marauders seized his horse, but luckily he had a purse under each arm and these he faithfully saved for his master and returned intact.

17.   After arriving, Pulaski had a meeting with the Pasha in command of the garrison, but this man did not greet him kindly at all, being informed about our little tussle with the Turks; and we could not count on his protection. That is why our Marshal [Pulaski] having recovered his money decided to go immediately at his own cost to Stanbul and there through the intervention of the French representative work something out with the Divan [Turkish authorities] so that we would have food and living quarters; as it was not fit to continue being a burden on our very kind Christians. In this journey (for which the Pasha gave him permission and an open letter) I was to accompany him, but God decreed otherwise, striking me with an illness which was a fever with the shivers and for three days I was in bed with a headache and shakes. Like it or not I had to stay and Pulaski took Bohdanek to Stanbul along with his Dragoman, that is interpreter.

18.   A Venetian doctor prescribed some powder that was as bitter as absinthe and told me not to consume food, especially fish, cheese or eggs. After a few days of this therapy, the fever abated somewhat, the attacks were shorter and less intense. Because the weather was beautiful I, Mazowiecki and Wielichowski walked about the city admiring various buildings especially the great mosque or Turkish church, built of fine materials and funded at great expense by Sultan Selim. It has a powerful many minarets all straight and tall like candles, surrounded by galleries and so delicately wrought in stone that they seem translucent and appear as if, looking from the bottom, they were made of ruffles of Belgian lace. We went also into the fields, reaching even some of the nearby villages. The soil is rich and fertile but the farms are neglected; because the Turks just love fruit and vegetable gardens, and don't care much to plant grain. Here and there you see a bit of wheat, barley or corn, the rest lies fallow. But the gardens are beautiful, full of orange and fig trees — and in the rows are vegetables, mostly onions, cucumbers, and sweet pumpkins.

19.   From a Frenchman we learned some interesting things. That is: all the peasants in the vicinity of Adrianopol are descended from Ruthenian folk of Podole and Ukraine, who during the Turkish wars were taken into *iassyr* [bondage] with their wives and children and forced to settle there. These people have become Moslems and forgot their beginnings. When Mazowiecki (who knew Turkish quite well) talked with them, they shook their heads with disbelief. But they don't speak the pure Turkish speech using many words from their former dialect. They

call their homes not *hane* but *chata*; father is *batko*; and a wife is *zona*. These words are all that remain as a heritage from their unhappy fathers. Our hearts would break when we saw this strange result of barbarian invasions and our near-brothers forced with violence from the Christian faith and now ignorant of their beginnings despite those crumbs of remembered speech, which without their knowledge remain like the carved letters on a worn stone taken and carted far away from an ancient Roman monument!

20.   After nearly a month of absence, Pulaski to my great joy returned from Stanbul. He brought good and bad news, mostly bad, such as is usual in the world. The French representative Monsieur de Saint-Priest received him most courteously and helped him gladly. Under his influence the Divan allocated funds and support to us, and sent us to the garrison town of Rodosto, located on the Marmara Sea, twenty some miles from Stanbul and nearly as far from Adrianopol. We had to go there. The political news were as follows: the Turks were much frightened and wanted an armistice from Rumiancow. He agreed but on condition that negotiations take place immediately and he sent Repnin to Sylistrya to make peace with the Turkish plenipotentiaries, but under conditions most unfavorable to the Porte. Nothing was said about the condition of the Rzeczpospolita in Europe. None of the powers made any protest. The cabinet at Versailles washed its hands of it, not wanting to get involved. The French representative was most embarrassed when speaking of this to Pulaski. Our entire hope was put upon Turkey, which unfortunately, during he rule of the new Sultan (for I forgot to say previously that Mustapha, the great ruler who was so well inclined toward Poland, died a year ago, and his place was taken by Abdul-Hamet) did loose its influence. After the last campaign against Russia, it was forced to adopt the sad alternative.

21.   I was loath to leave Adrianopol and the house of our dear Mr. Arnoux, for truth be told, I fell in love with the younger of his daughters, Marie. But what to do, when a man was still young and the girl was very pretty — and when one is in sadness, the heart tends to love all the more. So, for some unknown reason love found me during my French lessons and so captured me that from a resolute man I became timid, as if ashamed of myself, especially in the presence of those who knew my normal attitude. As far as I could tell the young lady did return my affection and if not for this departure, who knows how this would have ended — perhaps at the altar. But God ordained it otherwise! At the farewell

there was sadness aplenty; dear Marie had tears in her eyes and I, may God be my witness, was ready to weep but held back bravely, for what would people think if a Captain of the Confederates, a cavalier, would cry like an old woman or a school child.

22.   Rodosto is a town that is not large, but quite dirty, with a small guard castle at the edge of the sea — but its port is quite busy. Merchants, sellers, sailors of various nationalities, move to and from each trading in his own fashion. The commandant was not some cocky Pasha (as in the large cities) but one of the Sultan's lesser officers named *Beglir-Bey*. He had already received orders from Stanbul as to our disposition. He put us up in a large empty government building and paid us an allowance that had been sent up from the capital by the *Kisnadar-Aga*, that is the treasurer general. These quarters were used by the poor among us, but we, who still had some cash left, hired lodgings in the city, in the homes of Christians. We were very bored in Rodosto. Our only entertainment was walking on the seashore and looking at this natural wonder that is quite foreign to Poles (especially to those, like me, who had never sailed on grain barges to Gdansk). We collected seashells and other water curiosities; and were amused by looking at the exercises performed by the Turkish military, from which we had much laughter. It was like this. There was an artillery unit and they set up a small cannon outside the town for practice, and started shooting at a target pained on a board and propped up against a rock outcrop some distance away. We could see that one shot after another was hitting the outcrop three yards away, not the target. What did these impatient Turks do? They moved the target to the place where the cannonballs were striking and started to fire again. But now the shots went farther to the left, one even landing in the sea. Then they stopped firing and returned to their fort with drawn faces. We had a good laugh, but not too loudly, for these Moslems might have aimed the cannon at us, and their aim might have been better than at their target.

23.   Meanwhile, a treaty between Turkey and Russia had been signed in Kaynardzia, in Rumiancow's tent and was unfavorable to the Sultan because he had to recognize the independence of Crimea, give Russians the right to unimpeded sailing on the Black Sea and pay reparations of forty-million from his treasury. In this treaty there was no mention of Poland, and Repnin demanded that the old conventions, guaranteeing the sovereignty of the Rzeczpospolita, be canceled, and this was agreed to. So our last hope faded when Turkey, our last protector, forsook our

cause. Now only Almighty God could lift us out of the situation and save us from the disaster! We stayed in Rodosto for a while, desperate, making various plans but this was for naught. The beginning of the Year of Our Lord 1775 saw us in the same place — wondering what to do. Sad news came from all sides, while the indifference of the world made it even harder to bear for those suffering persecution. What went on in our souls then could be understood only by one who had gone away from his family to a foreign land and cried over the fate of his homeland, not being able to give it any help or solace.

24.　　Various plans, discussions and councils — but mostly poverty (for the allowances given us were small) — convinced us that we should consider returning home, for some said that they would waste away here and perhaps even turn Moslem. Therefore Mazowiecki, in the name of the group, composed a petition to Poniatowski in writing and sent it to Warsaw where it was delivered to the king. All this was done with Pulaski's knowledge and consent, who made no protestation against the king but did not sign this submissive document. He never asked for any favors or forgiveness for himself. Wielichowski, because of his friendship with the Marshal, and I because of duty, followed his example, promising to share his fate come what may, for which he thanked us sincerely. A few months later came a favorable reply from Warsaw; so our fellow sufferers already tired of the daily view of the sea and grown thin on Turkish cucumbers and corn, gladly departed for Poland while I and Pulaski left Rodosto for Stanbul. This took place at the end of November 1775.

Book Eight

Stay in Stanbul - Sailing to France - Toulon - Paris - Visit with Benjamin Franklin - Ship journey and arrival in America

1.　　Stanbul is a large city, and from afar (especially from the water) is unutterably beautiful; but when you enter inside there is a different world. Except for the palaces of the Sultan, the military barracks, and the Bazaars where the merchants ply their trade — it is a city of wooden buildings, small without windows and porches. The narrow streets are teeming with dogs, donkeys, horses and Turkish ragamuffins — dirty and ragged, like our Polish Jews. There is the stench of corruption in the air and deadly vapors which no doubt helps to spread the plague. In the Christian quarter it is seemingly better and tidier, but not much. In a word, Stanbul can be admired but one must hold one's nose and look at it from afar; only then can one see the white towers and the domes of the mosques which are very fine structures, and when the sky above is fair and of a dark blue hue — then the landscape is eerily attractive. For our quarters we hired a small house with a garden which Monsieur Arnoux had for the use of visiting officials and let us use for a time. It was a bit small, but peaceful and at least the odors and foulness of the city did not reach us.

2.　　We stayed in Stanbul about thirteen months and had the time to see practically everything; except two things: the inside of a mosque (where *giarow* or Christians are not allowed) and the face of a Turkish lady. These go on the streets so wrapped as to only have a slit to see through. This custom is not because of any timidity or modesty on the part of the ladies, but because of the great jealousy of the bearded Turks. While we were bored, among our favorite pleasures was the company Monsieur de Saint-Priest, a fine and very courteous man, as are all the French. He was a great admirer of our country, and had heard much about Pulaski also reading about him in the newspapers, thus he was sincerely friendly and considerate toward him. Being often with this gentleman, I had ample opportunity to converse and improve my French language to perfection. Only Wielichowski, though not particularly hard-headed, could not master this language, and spoke better Turkish than French.

3.   Time galloped by and we had to spend money to live — thus the funds that Pulaski had were much diminished; my money belt half emptied. It was getting lean, with the future ahead looking unhappy, cold and hungry. Therefore Wielichowski decided to go back to Poland where a general pardon had been announced for the Confederates (except for the highest commanders). Taking advantage of a merchant caravan to Brodno, he departed with them. He bade farewell to me and Pulaski, placing us under the protection of Almighty God. It was sad to see our companion go, especially since he was departing not from lack of determination but, as he secretly told me, not to be a burden to Pulaski. This took place in October of the Year if Our Lord 1776.

4.   Monsieur de Saint-Priest received French newspapers where there was always fresh news of happenings in the world. But the most noise in Europe was caused by the rebellion of the American Colonies against the English, that started over a year ago because of heavy taxes, and other injustices, force and violence. The American Congress, that is their Sejm, named George Washington as commander in chief, a man of great energy and military talent. He took steps against the enemy and had a few successes. The French had been enemies of the English for uncounted years and always looked askance at that power. They were happy over this diversion, but only in private, for the French government did not want yet to become embroiled in this matter, but later did (about this later). Monsieur de Saint-Priest spoke with great affection and praise about the Americans fighting for freedom against English tyranny. This got Pulaski excited and he decided to cross the ocean to reach that country — and offer his services.

5.   I was not against this, being fully determined because I was bored from sitting uselessly and looking at minarets and day-dreaming. But to make the journey required the most important thing — that is money. Here the providence of God intervened, as it often does among sinful men; and a miracle saved us from the situation. After dinner I was resting on the sofa with Pulaski, smoking pipes and discussing our forthcoming journey, wondering whether to approach the Divan for aid or ask France for a subsidy. I heard that Bohdanek was speaking with someone in the anteroom. I went there and saw a man dressed not in the Moslem fashion, but like a Greek, speaking the dialect that Christians use in Stanbul, that is broken French (which is the language of the Franks). He asked if a Polish gentleman named Pulaski was there. I replied in the affirmative and he told me that banker Zizinia would

like to have Monsieur Pulaski come and get his dinars — that is money. Pulaski was most surprised when I told him and tried to imagine who would have sent him some cash; after which we went to see the banker.

6.   Zizinia said that Tepper, a Warsaw banker, sent him two thousand red zlotys with the command that they be handed over to Pulaski personally; and to obtain a receipt. When we asked from whom this money was sent he could not answer. Pulaski had some reluctance about accepting these ducats given by an unknown hand; yet I persuaded him that they were not a present either from the Russian Tsarina or Poniatowski. Thus, he would not soil his hands or burden his conscience by accepting them. He accepted this argument and took a sum that was most helpful to us. Back then, or even now, I was at a loss to learn who was our anonymous donor and benefactor — but always suspected that it might have been Prince Radziwill, also known as *Panie Kochanku* [My Dear Sir] (who was by no stretch a savant and barely could sign his own name; but he did love our country and did help his brother nobles in need, especially patriots); or another magnate who was not connected to the St. Petersburg cabal (but truth be told there were few such and those could be counted on the fingers of one hand).

7.   After we got the money all went smoothly. Monsieur de Saint-Priest praised the idea of our journey and informed us that recently an American plenipotentiary, one Franklin, a fine and learned man, arrived in Paris to look after the interests of his country and send volunteers back across the sea. So the Frenchman advised us to sail from Stanbul to Toulon and from there travel to Paris to obtain information and advice on how to continue our noble enterprise. The French representative also gave Pulaski a letter to his older brother (who had the title of Count and a position at the court in Versailles) with a very friendly recommendation to him. We sailed from Stanbul on February 4 Year of Our Lord 1777 under the protection of God and the Holy Patron Saints in whom we had our Christian faith. Before departure Pulaski, in both our names, wrote a most courteous farewell to Monsieur Arnoux and his family. At the end I appended a few sweet and sincere words for my Marie, whom, unfortunately, I would never see again.

8.   The voyage lasted nearly two months due to unfavorable winds. Meanwhile I was able to see many natural wonders and interesting sights. First the famous Dardanelles, a very strong military position and the archipelago of islands settled by the Greeks, sitting on the blue sur-

Karol Stanislaw Radziwill by (1734 - 1790) by Konstanty Aleksandrowicz, 1786

face of the sea like a flock of ducks or swans. Further on were the shores of Italy and Vesuvius — the fiery mountain at whose peak smoke is always belching like a chimney of a smelter (they say this fire-mountain sometimes throws fire and coals but this we did not get to see). Our ship also crossed between Scylla and Charibdis, these two monsters which from the time of Ovid have been peaceful and no longer bother travelers — so we passed them by unharmed. At last the shores of France came into view and we entered the port of Toulon where we were immediately taken and bathed in vinegar to remove any traces of the Turkish contagion. Seeing that we had no defect they let us go. The commander of the garrison, to whom Pulaski also had a letter, received us kindly and speaking of this and that, told us among other things, that a young Pole named Koszuko had left Toulon for America at the end of the previous year.

9.   For some time we strained our brains to recall who that Pole with the strange name might have been, but only after reaching America did we find out it was Thaddeus Kosciuszko, the same one who later would gain such great fame in both hemispheres. Since most may not be aware of the original reason for Kosciuszko's leaving Europe, I'd like to include the following story, given by reliable witnesses. It was like this. Kosciuszko was stationed in Lithuania with his regiment and fell in love with the daughter of the Great Marshal Jozef Sosnowski. The young lady took his attentions kindly, he declared himself asking the parents for the honor of becoming their son-in law. Sosnowski, wealthy and proud, answered sourly "Turtledoves are not for sparrows, and magnates' daughters are not for the petty nobles." The two lovers, feeling themselves mistreated, decided to elope; and attempted to do so. But they were overtaken two miles down the Grodno road by Sosnowski's men. They seized the lady and because the young man tried to defend her; they beat him and left him wounded and bleeding in the road. After this adventure, which caused much furor in the Great Kingdom and the Royal Lands, a desperate Kosciuszko resigned and went to America.

10.   Between Toulon and Paris the chief cities are: Marseilles famous for trade and beautiful port buildings; Avignon, a possession of the Pope, where at a hilltop church we saw with awe the tombs of two popes beautifully made of marble; Lyon, or the French Lwow [Lion town] located on two rivers where they manufacture silk cloth and ribbons, so prized by our ladies. But we easily forgot about these places after we reached Paris. Here was a city above all cities! What impressive buildings, what

a richness of costume, in carriages, in harness. What motion, what merriment! Stanbul and all the German towns can go and hide. This is real life! Here's something that animates a man and forces him to act. If you took Lot's wife, the one that became a pillar of salt, and planted her on a Paris street, she would have come alive and ran to laugh and make merry with the others. We stopped at a decent tavern, under the sign of a swan, on a river near a great masonry bridge that they call *New Bridge*, but it looked pretty old to me.

11.   In Paris at the time there were a few of our Confederates including the steward Wielhorski and starosta Miaczynski. Pac was also in France but he was in Strasbourg on the German border. Miaczynski lived large and in a fine house, not far from the church where the body and heart of our king Jan Kazimierz are buried. He knew many French dignitaries, was attached to the court at Versailles and had hopes of getting an army commission. He took Pulaski to Monsieur de Saint-Priest, who on reading his brother's letter, received him most kindly and offered him his help in all things. Learning that we intended to sail for America he introduced us to a handsome young man from a good home, Monsieur de Noailles, who a month ago was ready to make this very journey, but was diverted due to difficulties. Knowing the American agents, he promised to take us to them, a promise that was soon kept.

12.   There was much talk in France then about the escapades of a young officer who belonged to one of the finest families, the Marquis de Lafayette a relative of Monsieur de Noailles. He left his family, a young wife, and equipping a ship secretly, sailed to America to fight the English. The king was most angry, the family lamented, and there was all kinds of talk in the court; but public opinion was on the side of the young man and his noble determination. In general, I'll say in parenthesis, that all the French cheered for the Americans. News about what success Washington was having against the English was quickly snatched up from newspapers or private letters. Since we were going to be involved in this war, we were received everywhere with the greatest consideration.

13.   A few days after our arrival we were found at our tavern by one Lazowski who claimed that he had been in the Confederation, but after listening to him, it seemed that he was not in any regiment and never took part in battle. Instead this young blade went adventuring and made it as far as Paris where he was having a fine time, because he liked to

drink and dance. After giving him some money we let this bird go, because I never liked the looks of him for he looked to be an impulsive man and some bad light shone from his eyes. That day Miaczynski gave us a fine dinner inviting Monsieur de Noailles and a few other Frenchmen from among the top nobility. Among them was Dumourier, our old acquaintance. Since relations between him and Pulaski were not quite straightened out, and I was never his admirer, few words were exchanged. The victuals were practically Polish and there were many toasts at the end: including the health of Washington, Lafayette and to the success of the Americans. The French government was being constantly admonished by their representative. Lord Stormont, and forbade any public displays in this vein, but as this was a private party, it could not interfere. Anyway this was being done everywhere.

14.   On the 5th or 6th of May Monsieur de Noailles took us by carriage to Passy, a village outside Paris, where lived the American agents: Benjamin Franklin and Silas Deane. We stopped at a small house surrounded by a garden, on a hill near a river. That day Deane was in Paris and Franklin had gone out for a walk, so we were alone with the secretary Mr. Carmichael. He told us that Franklin would be back soon, for he had been out walking for nearly two hours. In a few minutes the door opened and an older gentleman came in leaning on a cane. He was serious looking, grey and with a very pleasant and open face. This was Franklin, the famous savant who with the help of science found a way to protect against lightning; now he had to find a way to protect his country from the tyrannical English. Later, I saw a portrait of this famous American with the following note: *Eripuit coelo fulmen, sceptrumque tyrannis.* [He took lightning from heaven and the scepter away from the tyrant] The words may be a bit sinful, but the concept is good.

15.   Franklin was quite good at speaking French, better than his secretary. Learning who we were and our intentions; he shook our hands very hard after the custom of his country and was very happy to have met us. He asked Monsieur de Noailles about Lafayette but the answer was that besides a letter written from the Spanish port from which he departed, there were no further news of him. "We need such people (said Franklin), people with a warm heart and noble attitude. I expect that you Polish gentlemen, who have such a reputation as great warriors will be of help to our poor country." To this Pulaski said: "Our nation has a particular dislike toward all tyrants, especially foreign ones — so then wherever there is a fight for freedom anywhere on the globe, it is

also our cause." The old man liked this response very much, he said also that in the first days of June a ship will sail from Havre to America with weapons, ammunition and a few volunteers on which we may travel. He asked us to keep this a secret, adding that the English representative had many spies, who in Paris, and especially in Passy, went about like bloodhounds, sniffing and tracking the intentions of the friends of American independence.

16.   We also had news about our homeland. From Wielhorski and Mialczynski we learned that after the unhappy partition, a movement started in the now smaller country to get organized and think about introducing some order. As the saying goes: "a Pole is only wise after he suffers a loss." This wisdom has at last come to stay. The public treasury has been reinforced by money from new taxes and offerings freely given; attention was directed to writing new laws and organizing a national system of education. The weakling Poniatowski straightened up, promoting education; and fine scientists, and writers appeared giving some luster to the nation. Unfortunately, outside its borders Poland was not being given any political consideration. This saddened us greatly in Paris where all the European powers, and even the smaller German and Italian principalities, had representatives — Poland had none. The French king did not send an ambassador to Poland, but supposedly had an agent in Gdansk to help the merchants from his country.

17.   We had a fine time of it, touring all the interesting places in Paris and the vicinity; beautiful churches, rich palaces with gardens, where are wonderful fountains and statues of marble and copper so finely wrought that they seem alive. This was especially true in Versailles where Louis XVI lived with his young Austrian wife and the entire court. We also went outside the city to a famous factory that manufactured porcelain whiter than that made in Saxony [Dresden] which is painted in strangely wonderful patterns; not only waves and flowers (like at home or in Turkey) but human figures from present or past history. We were always being invited to dinner, by Monsieur de Saint-Priest, Monsieur de Noallies and other persons, who received Pulaski with friendship and respect. To attend such receptions we obtained karabellas [Polish sabres] and traditional Polish clothes, which the French (used to their short jackets and stick-like swords) had reason to admire.

18.   Pulaski often went to Passy, with me or by himself, to deliberate with the Americans who had grown to like him very much for his stance

and cavalryman's determination. Deane, a provident and clever man, once told us in confidence that things were going well; that the court at Versailles was quietly getting ready to go to war against the English, and would try to get Spain as an ally. The last time we visited them was on May 29 on which day Franklin and Deane, on parting with us, gave letters to us for Washington and a request directed at the captain of their ship, that he should give us passage. Monsieur de Noailles wrote to his relative, the Marquis de Lafayette, for whom we were to take news from his wife, a young and pretty lady. Having these recommendations in hand, we bade farewell to our friends and on the following day went to the port city of Le Havre.

19.   Having set sail on the open sea in a ship called *La belle Louise*, that is Beautiful Louise, we started looking at our companions. In addition to the captain and crew there were five French volunteers, but they were not much to speak of, rather inauspicious fellows. One of them, named Girod, seemed to be valiant, but turned out to be a braggart. This man, with graying hair and a tanned faced, had wandered across the world. He served in the Seven Years' War in an Austrian dragoon regiment. Not being able to stay in one place he went to St. Petersburg to seek a commission and rubles; later he changed his mind and came to France having no possibility of getting a position — decided to go to America, hoping to find mountains of gold. If all he said was true, this Girod would have been quite the hero; but he over praised himself and we know that a cow which moos too much, gives little milk. He was a Gascon, and people from that province (as the French say among themselves) are very talkative but cowardly also.

20.   In Paris, Pulaski and I purchased English grammars and lexicons with English vocabularies (for the Americans use this language in conversation), so that during travel we could study the language. The first word that Pulaski found was *forward* which in Polish is *naprzód*, very necessary when giving commands. Slowly, day by day, we complied a list of the most important words in our heads. Though this was the season most favorable to sailing, we had contrary winds and bad storms, during which it seemed that judgement day was nigh, for the waves were surrounding the ship on all sides and it seemed they would swallow it up. Our friend Girod, the resolute warrior, went white in such moments, and one could see that he had fear under his collar. I must also admit that these water dances were not to my liking at all. Only Pulaski

kept a steady countenance and a calm eye when looking upon the fury of the raging ocean.

21.   The regions which we traversed are very hot and we were bothered by heat and it seemed that live fire was gushing from the heavens. The water in barrels began to spoil, and for food we only had dry bread and salted meat; not the best of fare. To save our bellies the captain decided to stop at an island in the possession of the French king, called Saint-Domingue, where were most glad to get ashore. Only here one can tell one is not in Europe, as there are different trees, animals and birds; while most of the people are black like coal, that is Negroes. Their faces seemed to have been disfigured by nature, and the Europeans living there use them for the heaviest work, worse than oxen or horses. These black unfortunates, both men and women, go about practically naked, at most wrapping an apron about their middle. Shame is totally unknown in this land; the dissipation is great and an offense unto to God.

22.   On this interesting island, where we remained for a week, a sad incident took place which did much sadden myself and Pulaski. It was like this. Our dear and faithful Bohdanek, who was an excellent swimmer and loved water exercise; was bathing near the shore and went swimming out into the depths where he was eaten by a sea monster, called a *requin* [shark] in this land, a kind of sea-wolf. Pulaski then said: "This is an ill omen, my friend!" And later it did come true (about which I will later write). But Pulaski did not fall into desperation and I, not expecting anything, calmed down. For pleasure, or rather amusement, I would go hunting with a flintlock, shooting at the screaming monkeys or the birds whose plumage was so beautiful to behold that I was truly sad at having to kill these fine birds.

23.   Taking on food and fresh water, as much as was needed, we departed from Saint-Domingue. The remaining segment of the voyage was short but dangerous, for along the shores of the colonies the English have stationed their war ships to catch any ships that would bring aid to the rebels. That is why our captain, knowing full well of this danger, maneuvered carefully as not to fall into their hands. We were to make land as close as possible to Philadelphia, where the American Congress was meeting and were Washington was camped with his army. Such was our intent and the captain carefully looked through a long telescope to spot any danger. Fortunately, we were near the shore when a storm broke out and drove us back, but it must have also scattered the English

picket ships. For this reason, after the wind died down, we steered for the shore and with the setting sun stood on American soil, giving thanks to God that we had reached the end of our voyage. This happened on August 20, Year of Our Lord 1777. And thus the promise I gave to Pulaski five years ago at Częstochowa came true when I said *I would go even to the Antipodes with him.* I had no idea then that we would go that far, but it happened and we were in the Antipodes, on the other side of the earth's globe.

24.   We landed in some poor village near the mouth of the Delaware where our captain, well versed in English, learned from the inhabitants that General Washington with his army was encamped at Wilmingtown near Philadelphia about 20 miles from where we were. There we went after resting. Right after arriving I wanted to try out my knowledge of English and impress others with the fluency of the vocabulary which I had learned, but no one person could understand me, nor I anyone else. The reason was as follows: the English language is pronounced differently from that which is written and is more difficult than French. Here was the error and our useless effort. But the Americans don't even speak Latin, so initially it was difficult to converse with them.

Book Nine

American Army Camp - Washington, First meeting with the English - Pulaski named Brigadier General - Winter Quarters at Trenton - Thaddeus Kosciuszko - Intrigues and personal disputes - Pulaski resigns command and forms separate corps - Small skirmishes - Charlestown

1.   In Wilmingtown there were about nine thousand soldiers living in huts made of branches and set in several lines. From a distance it looked like a great village, but surrounded by an earthen wall and moat. On first sight, the American army did not impress me at all, having no uniforms and seeming like a rabble. Most of the soldiers wore grey jackets, others had canvass coverlets. Some had boots, others shoes, and some were barefoot. In sum not much of an army but rather rag-tag and if not for the muskets and cartridge boxes it was more like a crowd of simple peasants. That was my first impression, but later when I saw these ragamuffins under fire and fighting back bravely, I changed my mind and gained some respect for them. Pulaski also said, "They have no boots, but they have heart — and with that, my brother, you can go far, even barefoot!"

2.   We found the Marquis de Lafayette, who was most happy to get a letter from his wife. After reading the writing from his relative, Monsieur de Noailles, he received us in the French manner — that is most courteously, nobly and sincerely. He was at a loss as to where to sit us and was most attentive to us. He immediately took us to the quarters of the American commander, George Washington, who also had a hut; though bigger than the others it was modest without any wall hangings or other unnecessary decorations. I looked with interest and admiration at this man about whom all Europe had been talking loudly for three years; who was so loved and respected by his subordinates and the American nation. Then Washington might have had about 45 years. He was tall, broad shouldered, of fine build and pleasant of face. His clothing was proper but not showy, without any bangles or embroidery. It seemed that the American agents in Paris praised us greatly for after he looked at their writings, he greeted us with consideration asking whether we would like to serve in the cavalry or the infantry? Pulaski

said that he grew up in the saddle, and that Poles have an inborn desire to ride — and he would prefer to be assigned to the cavalry. It happened that the colonial cavalry was without a commander, as General Reed did not want this duty. So Washington stated he would write to Congress and propose that this job be given to Pulaski.

3.   Everyday more adventurers would arrive from Europe and all wanted high rank, that is why not everyone was accepted. The fact that Washington gave us such distinctions created much envy among the French who had been turned away. Most angry was Girod who had not been accepted — but as he made a large protestation, yelling and lamenting, he was given some money to see him on his way. Franklin and Deane, seeing us in Paris among Dukes, Marquises and other nobles gave us titles of Count, that the Germans call Graff, turning us into Count Pulaski and Count Rogowski. It is true enough that every noble born in Poland is a candidate for the crown, thus having a greater potential than the highest of the nobles abroad — so we let them give us these titles after they learned about our abilities. Pulaski's name gave the Americans little trouble in pronunciation, but mine they just could not manage, twisting it around and calling me Kokoski, or Kolkoski, but never Rogowski.

4.   I was given a hut near that of Lafayette, and there stayed for ten days waiting for Congress to make its decision. Then we got news from spies that the English generals Cornwallis and Howe, sailed from New York with a powerful contingent, and landed near Philadelphia threatening to take the city. So the Americans went out to greet their uninvited, but quite expected guests. The Marquis de Lafayette, Pulaski and I, though still not assigned to any command, went with the army as volunteers. On September 10 we met the enemy at the muddy shores of the Brandywine Creek, and a fight started. The colonists stuck green sprigs into their hats which created a strange but pretty sight; they advanced with vigor, and encouraged each other with merry shouts. It started with an artillery bombardment, switching to swords and bayonets. The well trained English regiments stood their ground like a wall, but our lines wavered and could not stand up to them, yet they fought bravely with true cavalier spirit. In this skirmish Lafayette was wounded in the leg; and I was struck in the head by a red-coated dragoon whom I quickly dispatched into the next world. My wound was not dangerous, he struck my hat and chopped off some skin with hair. But it was my poor head again, and speaking in parenthesis, from the time of the battle in Lomza

(of which I already wrote), when a cossack stuck it with a pike, it was damaged on nearly every occasion. But in all my life no other part sustained injury.

5.   Retreating after sustaining losses and moving toward Philadelphia, Washington received messages from Congress, and among them was the appointment of Pulaski as Brigadier General and of me as Major of Cavalry. Each of us took over his command, eager to act and show the Americans what two Poles could do. A few days after fording the Schuylkill river, the two armies met again, but rain interfered and drove the two groups apart. For forty-eight hours it rained by the bucketful and we were drenched to the skin. All the ammunition was wet, turning into a black paste. But the English got just the same, so were not able to attack us, nor we them. But they did maneuver to get behind us but this did not work as Washington was alert, having eyes not just for show. The difficulties, however, were many in marching through the forests, wetlands, and crossing rivers, of which there are many in this country, all wider than the Wisla [Vistula] or Niemen.

6.   Moving always toward Philadelphia, on October 4 Washington came upon about a thousand English in a fortified position at Germantown, and decided to attack them. It rained that morning, then there was fog during the attack. Moreover, our General Conway (an Irisher by birth) who led the left wing, sent his riflemen — that is the choice sharpshooters — forward and struck at the redoubts which were not built up too high. In the beginning the thing went well. Pulaski and his dragoons rode through the camp striking at anyone who got in their way, so that I saw his blade covered with blood. I did not let up, and my head managed to come through unscathed. But then the English counter-attacked and chased us far. During the battle Cornwallis brought up a great force and after breaking up our right flank turned on us. Our first two battles on American soil did not go well; but as they say nothing ventured — nothing gained; third time pays for all. In any case we did our duty, so there was no burden on our consciences. Congress, after this defeat moved quickly out of Philadelphia. The English took the city; while the American army, after much marching, stood camp about twenty miles away, at a place called Valley Forge, among the forests, near the Schuylkill river.

7.   It was well that among all these misfortunes there came some good news. The American General Gates totally defeated the English

Casimir Pulaski as a general in the Continental Army by Arthur Szyk

General Burgoyne and on October 17 accepted his surrender at Saratoga. The eight-thousand man corps lay down its arms putting itself at the mercy of the victors. This news improved the morale of the nation, for hearts were beginning to sink low down toward the heels; so that even we foreigners felt the shame. At that time Pulaski and his command was sent to Trenton on the other side of the Delaware River, to the town of Trenton were we were quartered until the next spring. Now is the time to tell about the American cavalry. It consisted of two regiments, one composed of dragoons, the other of riders — together not quite four-hundred men. The first regiment was so-so, but the second was total rag-tag, not unlike Zbikowski's band. Neither had any practice in maneuvering; military regulations and following orders was about as well known as the *Our Father* among the Turks.

8.   So, Casimir Pulaski, stuck in winter quarters decided to put his command in order and teach these soldiers the proper exercises; but it was not easy to accomplish this honorable enterprise. The Colonel of dragoons (where I was appointed Major) was one Molens, a disagreeable man full of jealousy against the Poles. He found Captain Riganti, an Italian, as an assistant and the two of them started secretly spreading gossip against Pulaski among the officers and men. They were most angry about the fact that Pulaski made them post regular guards and continued to hold exercise maneuvers, in which (as was said) they had no talent at all and did not like; being wastrels used to drink and dissipation. Soon the two of us could understand English and caught onto their plotting and murmuring. As the Italian Riganti was most active in the intrigues, I called him Captain Intriganti. Pulaski seeing how things went, was not able to hide the truth and when someone went against him he would speak right up — so Colonel Molens had the truth explained to him in a hot way; and forced into submission.

9.   These misunderstandings and disputes depressed and annoyed Pulaski, and of these we had a few; with them we had other difficulties, shortages and misery. Often the army would have its pay held up and food was not delivered — and it was a bad winter, very intense frost — where our poor soldiers had nothing to eat or warm themselves with. We had to draw on our own funds as not to feel the hunger. But everything was most expensive, the locals not wanting to take our paper money, with which the Congress paid us. At last at the end of December, for the Christmas holiday we had some respite. Tadeusz Kosciuszko, serving as an engineer in the army up north, on the Canadian border, learned that

Pulaski was encamped in Trenton and came to visit us during his furlough. Kosciuszko did not have a mustache like Pulaski, but one could see on his face a noble kindness and openness. In addition he was a sweet man, full of news, so that his company and conversation was most pleasant. Though he was of equal age to Pulaski, they did not know each other in Poland (for the former was still at study when the latter was already fighting Russians). But here on foreign soil they met and did feel affinity to each other, swearing eternal friendship. After ten days of enjoyment, during which despite poverty we managed to eat like Poles, Kosciuszko returned to his corps and my eyes never again beheld him, not until the battle at Dubienka in 1792 (about which I will write later). I can say proudly, that in America I saw, not quite together, the three greatest heroes of my time: Washington, Pulaski and Kosciuszko; but I truly don't know which was the greatest.

10.   We stayed in Trenton unemployed until the first months of the Year of Our Lord 1778. Then at the end of February Pulaski received orders from General Wayne to make some forays into the vicinity of Philadelphia and get forage and cattle; to take these away from the English who were feasting in Philadelphia. We went out with a few dozen horses to do as ordered, and whenever we met the enemy and it came to a tussle we were always on top. Once, while with General Wayne we happened into the middle of a three thousand man corps; and our rear way was blocked, but we called upon God for help and cut our way through the surrounding English column. Here Pulaski showed what he could do; just as in Poland, here and now, he was in the first line on attack, and the last on retreat. He moved with grace and purpose, so that one was inspired just looking at him. His courage and awareness saved our small unit, and he came out of the fray with no harm, though his horse was wounded. Wayne could not find the words enough to praise him, while Washington on this occasion wrote him a letter of praise and affection.

11.   Arriving in Trenton we met Scudder, an officer of the dragoons, who had been given a furlough of fifteen days whereupon he spent two months with his family in Pennsylvania without permission. Pulaski then, to make an example, put the man under arrest. This upset the Americans who were being incited by the Italian Riganti, who said that they were fighting for freedom and here they were being tyrannized. Colonel Molens had him released taking the responsibility on himself. When Pulaski learned of this, never being one to let someone tweak his

noise, called the Colonel and in no uncertain terms dressed him down, sending him to the arrest. But this unruly man not only disobeyed the order but without anyone's say-so left town. Pulaski was most offended and sent a report to Wayne, requesting a court martial. The court met, but — what can be said — the Americans supported each other, and freed the Colonel. Pulaski saw in this as an affront to his honor and rank; immediately put in his resignation, asking for permission to sail to Europe — and he sent me with his letter to Valley Forge where the main headquarters was located.

12.   Washington read the letter and asked me for details, then understood how Pulaski was ill treated, but said that according to the law of this country he could not call another court-martial. He only added that it was sad that such a fine warrior, who had given ample proof of his courage, would leave the army at such a critical moment; but if he was resigning command of the cavalry why not take on another? I had no power to make any agreements, and telling him I did not know, took his response and returned to Trenton. Pulaski greatly respected Washington and would have been glad to do much as to make him content — as we say "that the wolf be sated, and the goat remain whole." In this way he would not have to quit the service and still retain his honor. After deliberating with me, Pulaski formed a project for creating a small independent corps, consisting of one-hundred riders and two-hundred foot, This would not be dependent on anyone and would conduct cossack-style warfare. After reporting to General Wayne and resigning our commands we left for Valley Forge. Washington liked Pulaski's plan and on March 28th it was accepted by Congress, then meeting in Yorktown. There were some objections when it came to the enlistment of deserters (Germans by birth who came to us in droves) but it was eventually allowed.

13.   We located ourselves in a place called Fishkill and started to form the legion. Pulaski did not want to have any American officers, so Frenchmen were sent to him, and among these, to command the infantry, was Colonel Armand (whose true name was Marquis de la Royerie, and I know not why he used only his Christian name). This Monsieur Armand, as is common to Frenchmen, was a most courteous gentleman and a determined cavalier, so we were on good terms with him as well as with all the other officers. Our uhlans, that the Americans called *lancemen*, had ling pikes with flags, and the infantry was given light equipment. Most of the soldiers were Hessians, tough looking men, not very agile but well schooled in obedience and in military maneuvers; so

General Anthony Wayne (1745 - 1796) by James Sharples Sr., 1795

General Benjamin Lincoln (1733 - 1810) by Charles Wilson Peale, 1784

it went as smooth as butter.

14.   Soon we received important news. The French king recognized the independence of the United States — and signed a treaty with its plenipotentiary on the day of February 6 in Paris. A fleet with ammunition and soldiers was sent under the command of Count d'Estaing, to give us aid. This happy event was celebrated with all indications of joy across he country. Washington wanted the army to show its sentiments and to this purpose sent instructions to all the commanders of corps and units. On the appointed day there were prayers — the army marched with its weapons, there were cannon salutes and the bands played. In the evening there was a plentiful meal with orders to have the soldiers shout "Long live the French king." Even our Hessians had to shout, though not so long ago they were trumpeting the praises of king George. This is how it is in this world — it you are riding on someone's cart, then you have to sing his song. The English, sensing what was afoot, sent emissaries to treat with Washington and made all possible concessions to the colonists. But Congress did not accept any of their proposals and it was well. Because two days after making this bold decision we received this good news from France.

15.   The English corps stationed in Philadelphia saw the threat presented by the French, so they marched out to the shore to board ships and go to New York where they would hide like mice in a hole. Washington understood perfectly the position in which the enemy would be, when they moved across swampy and forested terrain with their baggage and supplies. He ordered General Lee, as not to lose time (while he moved the main army) to harass the English during the march, not giving them time to rest, but continuously pick at their flanks and rear. We also received such orders to chase the enemy force (this was near the end of June) but the expedition was not successful because of slowness, stupidity, or betrayal by the General [Lee]. Some said that since Lee was an Englishman by birth, he should be under suspicion. A court-martial was convened over the fact that he had let the enemy go free, while he could have destroyed it or at least severely harmed it. He was put on suspension from command for a year.

16.   After this affair our legion was sent in pursuit of various bands commanded by English officers but consisting of wild Indians and *Tories* (as the sympathizers of the English king were called). These bands were like those found in the Ukraine and committed various crimes, violence and similar outrages — burning, robbing, and murdering innocent

people — not even letting children or dogs escape. The wild Indians (of whom it is said they eat human flesh) were painted up and dressed up in an unimaginable way, and were incredibly cruel toward the poor population — and teamed up with American rabble, made up a worthy combination. This rabble fought savagely and to the death for they knew that if they fell into our hands we would make short work of them. And so it was — no pardon was given to the enemy, and those that gave up were hung from the nearest tree. There was no shortage of branches in America, as it is a forested country.

17.   In general the war was fought fiercely on both side, no clemency being shown by either side. As both sides were Protestants, little can be said! Our legion had few Americans and all the officers were either Polish or French (the latter are not too pious, but after all are Catholics) so we did not go in for cruelties. We hung only the Tory leaders (for such was the order) letting the other prisoners go. In time Washington sent a new Pole, recently arrived from Europe, to our unit. He was named Jerzmanowski, a hardy and brave young man who brought us fresh news from Poland. He was most dutiful in his assignment on guard and during raids — so Pulaski grew to like him and predicted he would become an excellent warrior.

18.   During our time in winter quarters, not much new happened, except that once on a raid to Egg Harbor we were surprised at night by the English, who nearly wiped us out. On that occasion the vigilance of Pulaski and Colonel Armand saved the legion, so it was the attackers, having caused the alarm had to flee for their lives. They were ready to take us, but with God's help we chased them like a bunch of mangy old cats. The enemy who was once content to sit in New York and sometimes caused us trouble between the Schuylkill and Delaware Rivers, moved to continue the war in the American southern provinces, invading Georgia and the Carolinas. He took cities, burned villages and organized new bands of Tories under the leadership of Colonel Boyd; which committed much mayhem and violence on the innocent populace. Washington immediately sent General Lincoln with a strong force and in February in the Year of Our Lord 1779; Pulaski also got the order to join his command — so we traveled south.

19.   There was in Georgia, with the American militia, a preacher named Moyse Allen. Though Protestant he was a very determined, well spoken man, and a great patriot. Much was said about his praiseworthy deeds — how during the skirmishes he was always in the front line en-

couraging the men to fight; patching up the wounded, burying the dead, etc. I often heard Pulaski say: "Here's another Father Mark! I'd be glad, gentlemen, to know this brave soul and though he be an anti-papist, give him the praise he deserves!" But it was not to be. During a raid by General Prevost, this Reverend Allen was captured and the English put him aboard ship from whence he made an escape — but as he swam to shore his strength failed and he drowned. He was much mourned by the people.

20.   While making a rapid march to join General Lincoln's corps, already camped on the shores of the Savannah River, Pulaski learned that a strong English force was threatening the city of Charlestown, capital of Carolina. Since it was on our way, we went to relieve them, even though we were not asked. The city of Charlestown is solidly built; located on a peninsula that enters the sea so that it is surrounded by water on three sides. On the fourth side, from land, General Rutledge (in command of the local militia) burned down the houses in the suburbs and dug redoubts with a palisade, to use as a defense. On May eleventh, a thousand English soldiers crossed the Ashley River and set up camp opposite the fortifications. On the same day we crossed the Cooper River on a ferry (as in this country it can be said that there are more rivers than villages) and arrived at the city where we were greeted by General Multrie, a brave warrior and great admirer of Pulaski. The inhabitants, seeing our determined faces, gave us a feast.

21.   But Pulaski, not wishing to have Charlestown become our Capua [a military reference, not quite understood in this context], gave us only two hours to rest. Then he planned an expedition that was quite cleverly conceived. Usually in life he liked to be straight and open, but in war he would often use a stratagem and was happy to play a trick on his opponent, which Drewicz at Częstochowa had repeatedly tasted (as I already wrote above). The expedition was arranged as follows: Captain Fleury and one-hundred soldiers were stationed behind an embankment with orders to lay down on their bellies and not rise until the appropriate time. He and a cavalry unit, including myself and Jerzmanowski, were to approach the English camp and engage them for a moment — then pretend to flee toward the city. This was supposed to draw them into the trap, the way a young wolf is lured into a covered-over pit.

22.   Things went as Pulaski predicted. Seeing that our small unit was coming, General Prevost sent one-hundred horsemen in reply. We chased them this way and that, but without results on either side. Finally

Pulaski decided that he had the fish nibbling on the hook so we started to gallop away with the English behind us. It was still about a furlong and a half to the place where our people concealed. Pulaski said to me, "We'll get them, my brother, they will get caught in the trap." But Fleury, not waiting for the signal came out into the open and readied our men on the rise. "May ducks trample down that Frenchman, (shouted Pulaski in anger) he has spoiled my plan, that idiot." I looked around and saw that the English quickly understood what was up and gave up the chase. They turned about so quickly that we had no opportunity to go after them. Pulaski blamed Fleury, telling him without any reservation, that it was his fault. The Frenchman said that he thought he had heard the signal. And so the thing went wrong, but not because any fault of the Poles.

23.   The English General, not having any heavy cannon with him, decided to forgo any attack on the city and departed a few days later, placing his army on little islands along the shore, where he did much mischief and violence to the poor inhabitants; burning their homes with the livestock — killing defenseless old men, women and children. It was later said that these brigands even dug up graves looking for valuables in the coffins, and committed other acts of sacrilege on the dead. We soon started moving south toward General Lincoln to whose command (as I earlier stated) Congress had assigned us, and we reached him after a few days. The French fleet returned at the beginning of September from its expedition against English possessions in the Indies and was stationed off the Georgia shores. A plan was then conceived, to attack the city of Savannah from both land and sea, where the English were holed up in a fort.

24.   During this time the heat was unbearable, we were tired form continual marching; but solaced ourselves with the thought of taking a large town, of which all in the army were sure; because the combined forces of both countries were to act together against a common enemy. The French everywhere, even in America, are renown as a fighting folk; and Count d'Estaing left only sailors and gun crews aboard ship, taking all his infantry ashore and volunteered to lead the charge himself. There was no doubt of success! Pulaski was happy, he was making plans for the future, not expecting that his grave was to be here in Savannah on unhallowed ground, far from his beloved homeland; and that his death would be sudden, and without the sacraments... Just like a soldier. (About this I will write in the next book).

The death of Pulaski at Savannah

Book Ten

Storming the City of Savannah - Death of Pulaski - I resign and travel to Europe - Meeting at Saint Domingue with Bieniewski on his way to America - In Paris with Miaczynski - In Dresden with the Princess of Courland - Arrival in Poland

1.　　The City of Savannah is located on a river by this same name (near where it flows into the sea) which is a deep and wide, being able to accommodate ships. The city was open, only having a strong fortress on one side, furnished with redoubts and many cannon. On the other side the English put up several batteries and stationed soldiers. At the end of September (as I already said) the Americans came to Savannah with their French allies and sent a parley to General Prevost, asking him to surrender because he would not be able to withstand their force. The Englishman was clever and asked for twenty-four hours to think it over, stalling (as we learned later) to give General Maitland time to come with reinforcements; which took place. Then, our enemies feeling strong, laughed at the proposal and decided to have a battle. So we started to make the siege as per form. Our engineers dug trenches; the French ships moved in toward the shore. Meanwhile, the English made many forays. Twice they were repulsed with losses; but the third time they got better and killed many of our people.

2.　　Here I must mention one odd circumstance. I remember it as it were today, on first of October, seeing that Pulaski was out of sorts, I asked him at to what was the matter. "Oh, my brother (he answered me), yesterday I lost my scapular — and this is a bad omen." Pulaski, like all the knights was in solidarity, and wore a scapular touched to the miraculous icon of the Blessed Virgin which was blessed by the same Papal nuncio who visited us at Częstochowa (about which I already wrote). He was greatly saddened by this loss of a holy object which, as a true-believing Catholic, he treated with great piety. I tried to cheer him as I could and wanted to give him one of mine; but he declined not wishing to deprive me of this *heavenly shield* adding: "If such is the will of God, that here I must pay with my head; a sinful man may not stand against a verdict from on high; *fiat voluntas tua Domine* [let your will be done, Lord]." I was sad, but to tell the truth, I did not draw any prophecy from this; only later. Anyhow, Pulaski did not lament over this any longer, and on seeing this I stopped thinking about the incident.

3.   Four days later the bombardment of the fortress started, from the sea and land, but without any gain nor any great loss, on either side. A French Major named Lenfant behaved in a very brave manner; taking five soldiers with him and despite many shots being fired, sneaked up to the enemy fortress and set their palisade on fire; but the wood was rotten and the fire went out. Otherwise, we would have smoked them out like foxes from a burrow. On October 9th we were to make a general attack. The militia feinted an attack, but the main American and French forces went for the batteries located in a place called Spring Hill. It was hot there indeed — for over half an hour the cannons roared and blood flowed. Pulaski saw that there was an open space between the redoubts and decided to take a small unit of Georgia cavalry and break through there; get into the city and divert the enemy in this way. General Lincoln praised his bold plan. So calling on the help of God, Pulaski shouted *forward* and we, about two-hundred horse, followed him, galloping so that the earth thundered.

4.   The first two minutes went excellently well, we sped onward to perdition, but with grace, like noblemen. Only when we passed the two batteries between which the gap existed, we were halted by cross-fire and the entire group went into confusion like water that flowed quickly until it hit a closed sluice gate. I look — oh! Painful moment never to be forgotten! — Pulaski is on the ground. I raced over and dismounted rapidly, running to him, thinking the wound may be minor. But here was a great tragedy! A cannon ball had ripped his leg, and from his chest blood was also pouring forth, from another hit. When I knelt and started to raise him, he said with a deathly voice, "Jesus, Mary, Joseph." I heard nothing more nor did I see anything else for in that moment a musket ball slid along my skull, blood blinded me and I totally fainted. Our kind soldiers, urged by Jerzmanowski, retreating toward our lines bore away Pulaski and me (despite a lively fire), as well as other wounded. In the evening, after being bandaged by the medic, I regained consciousness, Jerzmanowski told me that Pulaski lived for yet another hour, but spoke deliriously as the ill are wont to do in fever — about Poland, about the future, and about someone named Franciszka! ... He asked that a cross with the figure of Jesus crucified be handed him, which he kissed and gave up his soul.

5.　　So he perished on this unfortunate day, October ninth of the year 1779, being not yet thirty-six years of age, the greatest Polish hero after Stefan Czarniecki. To properly remember and honor him one would need a writer like Virgil or someone as expressive as the Greek Plutarch. Here I am a military man, great of heart but not of intellect, more apt to grab a sword than turn to eloquence; could I create such a work? I will not be silent, but will tell it the best that I can. Pulaski greatly loved God, his homeland, and his fellow countrymen; he was courageous unto insolence and though of short stature, had an incredible strength in his hand — and fought with a sabre like none other. He never let anything slip by or fail to see it; he was rigorous in duty, and would not have forgiven his very brother a military blunder. He had no personal interests whatsoever, he did everything for the good of all; and would have shared his very last shirt gladly. In a word, his sentiments were chivalrous and beyond praise. He was a true Polish noble, as they say: "quick to anger, but wise at council; good for dancing and for serious matters; full of piety and steadfast in war." If he had a fault, it was that his blood tended to run hot and had no talent for dissembling; thus putting himself in offense and anger of others unintentionally![6]

6.　　After this unfortunate enterprise in Savannah during which our combined armies lost about a thousand men, Count d'Estaing — twice wounded — took his Frenchmen aboard ship and sailed away with God's grace. We, with General Lincoln, crossed a river and reached the province of Carolina. Command of our legion passed to Colonel Armand who was the senior officer. For me after Pulaski's death, though I healed from my wounds, everything seemed distasteful in America and I started to long for our home country; so much so I was unable to carry on, as a man whose body is well but who is injured and ill of mind. The loss of Pulaski, my companion of three years, a brother whom I loved, stuck a wedge into my heart and caused me unbearable sadness. Becoming an orphan, I now remembered where I was, an exile, and felt a

---

[6] Let us see how Lafayette, who knew Pulaski personally, spoke about our Bar Confederation cavalier. In the first volume of his memoirs published in Paris in 1837 after his death, we read on page 29: *Pulaski confedere polonais qui seul avait refuse sa grace: intrepide et vertueux chevalier - meilleur capitaine que general , il voulait etre polonais partout, et Monsieur de Lafayette apres avoir contribue a sa reception, travaillait souvent a ses raccommodements...* It is clear that *il voulait etre polonais partout* is wonderfully analogous to the words of Rogowski: *he was a true Polish nobleman.* And the frequent *raccommodements* signify that in Pulaski, as Rogowski says, *blood tended to run hot.* (Publisher's Note)

loathing toward those around me, and a longing for those who were far away!

7.   In truth, no fear of death drove me from America, for sinful man is born once, and dies once only. It is far better for a cavalier to finally close his eyes while in the saddle and under the clear sky, than to die in a feather bed behind a curtain. At least then one is spared the sadness and fear that is visited on the faces of one's friends and relatives. You need not be fed Latin prescriptions, and your body does not die by degrees. In war, one moment and all is done! And if you have not had a chance to confess your conscience and receive absolution and extreme unction — then there is God's mercy. ... ...

THE END

Publisher's Post-Script

Nearly seventy years have passed from the era in which these Memoirs end. The face of the old and new world has changed. New heroes have come and left the scene, leaving the luster of their fame on history's pages. Yet the memory of Casimir Pulaski that lives so strongly among us Poles is also preserved untouched in the hearts of the American people.

Ingratitude often lives in individuals, but in the collective nation, never! Nations always remember those who had sacrificed for the common good — those who in the defense of rights and freedom laid down that, which after honor was most precious — their lives!

That is why Pulaski has not been forgotten in the United States. His name lives in folk tradition and is still known; as is the name of Prince Jozef Poniatowski in France.

Our countryman Mr. Rudolf Gutowski spent a few years in the United States and made me happy with his stories of how Americans continue to remember our Bar Confederation cavalier.

In Georgia, between Savannah and Augusta is a small town called Pulaski; while a great many of the steamboats that travel among the southern provinces, also bear the name of this hero.

In the city of Savannah, in the main room of the City Hall, Mr. Gutowski saw a portrait of Kazimierz Pulaski that hangs there, painted in oil by a famous painter contemporary to the War of Independence; Mr. Stuart. In a square designated for public promenade, there is an obelisk of granite, and though it has no words engraved upon it, is called *Pulaski's Monument* by the city's inhabitants.

These details are small and of less significance — I place them here for the edification of all — because I am sure they will be pleasing to every Pole.

The blood spilled in the only cause of freedom is not lost; sooner or later each drop will yield a bountiful harvest; like fertile grain laid in the bosom of mother earth!

After so many years, many of our countrymen have wandered even to the New World — and even if among the cold (as European opinion would have it) American nation they can find a bit of sincere hospitality and real sympathy — then the cause of it, without denial are none other than the excellent services rendered by Tadeusz Kosciuszko and the death of Casimir Pulaski!

Konstanty Gaszyński

Konstanty Gaszyński (born on March 10, 1809, in Jeziornie and died on October 8, 1866, in Aix-en-Provence) - Polish poet, prose writer, publicist and translator. He came from an impoverished noble family, the son of Antoni Gaszyński and Teresa née Młynarski. A graduate of the Warsaw Lyceum. He studied at the Royal University of Warsaw. During this time, he made friends with Zygmunt Krasiński and visited the salon of his father, Wincenty Krasiński.

He participated in the November Uprising in the Lithuanian corps of Antoni Giełgud. He first emigrated to Belgium and then to France, finally settling in Aix-en-Provence. He later served as the tutor for the sons of Zygmunt Krasiński.

He started his publishing career in 1827 with a satirical poem in six songs, *Jaxsjada*. He translated French and German poetry as well as Serbian folk epics into Polish. He published several works in Poland, which included a poem in honor of Emilia Plater. He translated Polish literature (including *Anhelli* by Słowacki and *Przedświt* by Krasiński) into French as well as publishing original works such as Maciej Rogowski's Diaries. He collaborated with French magazines: Gazette du Midi and Memorial d'Aix, where he was the editor-in-chief.

Konstanty Gaszyński

A Legend According to Konstanty Gaszyński

Many excellent scholarly books have been written on the life of Casimir Pulaski. Two which head the list are Wladyslaw Konopczynski's "Kazimierz Pulaski Zyciorys" and Janusz Roszko's "Ostatni Rycerz Europy." But among the fictionalized life-stories of our Polish-American hero the one that tops the list as the all-time great is "Reszty Pamietnikow Macieja Rogowskiego" by Konstanty Gaszynski. It turned out to be a very popular book. The first edition was published in Poznan in 1847, the third in Lwow in 1888. There was also a French edition.

In the introduction the author explains that this is only a transcription of the remaining part of a memoir of his old friend Maciej Rogowski, whom he knew as a youth. The memoir was lost after his death and only recently found - what was left of it - hence the "remainder." Apparently, the red leather-bound book, the original handwritten manuscript, wound up in the pantry and whenever the cook was baking, she would rip out a page of parchment to line the pan.

The story, which has a distinctly authoritative and fluid narrative tone, indeed it seems so real that some historians have accepted it as factual and used it as a reference. Written in the style of Jan Chrystosom Pasek the book is entertaining not only with its vivid descriptions, action packed anecdotes, but also the picturesque old Polish language used.

The action begins at the time when Pulaski (whose name Gaszynski consistently spells "Puławski") is forced to give up the defense of the Częstochowa monastery and leave Poland. He leaves to the great sorrow of his compatriots and arrives in Turkey to fight the Russians. Here the focus of the story shifts to Rogowski, who can find trouble without any help whatsoever.

"It was well into the evening when we reached the bank of a small river where we intended to make our camp for the night. At this time a group of mounted Turks came toward us - about fifty men of their cavalry. As they reached us, they shouted threats, one being the loudest, yelling: *Issewa hazyr* at the top of his lungs. I asked Suski what was meant, and he says: "the man is calling you a Christian swine." Oh, wait you pagan! (I thought). And when he continued his insults, I was seized by impatience, my right palm itching something awful, I grabbed my saber and had at him. The Turk raised his weapon and we exchanged strokes. Then I struck him with great force, his head went down, and he fell from the saddle. Unfortunately, my impetuosity drew some unhappy consequences. The Turks, on seeing their companion slain, went at the Poles and we had an intense fight. I thought: "Now that I've brewed some bitter beer, at least I should have a drink" and went at them. The fight lasted about half-hour. Six of our men fell, among them Sulmirski, but there were twenty dead Turks without counting the wounded, and they withdrew. Then a new regiment came up, they took heart and were at us again. It was getting plenty hot, for now they had a swarm of about two-hundred while there were but thirty of us Poles. Fortunately, God's providence was with us for the commander of this new regiment was Osman Aga, Pulaski's friend who recognized us and stopped his men. When our interpreter explained things, how we were abused with insults and had to defend ourselves for no reason, the matter was settled! But this did not return life to our dear departed. We buried them decently, though without church ceremonies and in unhallowed ground."

Winding up their affair in Turkey, Rogowski and Pulaski travel through Germany to France. Along the way Casimir Pulaski fights a duel against another Pole who had slandered his name. We see a Pulaski who is both noble and idealistic as well as brave and impulsive. In the story he is a master swordsman as he probably was in real life. The duel ends after Pulaski has deftly sliced off his opponent's ear. Eventually the two companions make their way to France and meet Benjamin Franklin. The occasion is described in detail.

"On the 5th or 6th of May Monsieur de Noailles took us by carriage to Passy, a village outside Paris, where lived the American agents: Benjamin Franklin and Silas Deane. We stopped at a small house surrounded by a garden, on a hill near a river. That day Deane was in Paris and Franklin had gone out for a walk, so we were alone with the secretary Mr. Carmichael. He told us that Franklin would be back soon, for he had been out walking for nearly two hours. In a few minutes the door opened, and an older gentleman came in leaning on a cane. He was serious looking, grey and with a very pleasant and open face. This was Franklin, the famous savant who with the help of science found a way to protect against lightning; now he had to find a way to protect his country from the tyrannical English. Later, I saw a portrait of this famous American with the following note: *Eripuit coelo fulmen, sceptrumque tyrannis.* [He took lightning from heaven and the scepter away from the tyrant] The words may be a bit sinful, but the concept is good.

Franklin was quite good at speaking French, better than his secretary. Learning who we were and our intentions; he shook our hands very hard after the custom of his country and was very happy to have met us. He asked Monsieur de Noailles about Lafayette but the answer was that besides a letter written from the Spanish port from which he departed, there were no further news of him. "We need such people (said Franklin), people with a warm heart and noble attitude. I expect that you Polish gentlemen, who have such a reputation as great warriors will be of help to our poor country." To this Pulaski said: "Our nation has a particular dislike toward all tyrants, especially foreign ones - so then wherever there is a fight for freedom anywhere on the globe, it is also our cause." The old man liked this response very much, he said also that in the first days of June a ship will sail from Havre to America with weapons, ammunition and a few volunteers on which we may travel. He asked us to keep this a secret, adding that the English representative had many spies, who in Paris, and especially in Passy, went about like bloodhounds, sniffing and tracking the intentions of the friends of American independence.

Soon they board a ship for America and arrive - just south of Philadelphia. However, verifiable historical documents and letters describe Pulaski landing in the vicinity of Boston and then travelling south to meet with General Washington and his army encamped at Moland's House in Hartsville, PA - just a few miles from Doylestown where now stands the National Shrine of Our Lady of Częstochowa.

Taking on food and fresh water, as much as was needed, we departed from Saint-Domingue. The remaining segment of the voyage was short but dangerous, for along the shores of the colonies the English have stationed their war ships to catch any ships that would bring aid to the rebels. That is why our captain, knowing full well of this danger, maneuvered carefully as not to fall into their hands. We were to make land as close as possible to Philadelphia, where the American Congress was meeting and where Washington was camped with his army. Such was our intent and the captain carefully looked through a long telescope to spot any danger. Fortunately, we were near the shore when a storm broke out and drove us back, but it must have also scattered the English picket ships. For this reason, after the wind died down, we steered for the shore and with the setting sun stood on American soil, giving thanks to God that we had reached the end of our voyage. This happened on August 20, Year of Our Lord 1777. And thus, the promise I gave to Pulaski five years ago at Częstochowa came true when I said *I would go even to the Antipodes with him.* I had no idea then that we would go that far, but it happened, and we were in the Antipodes, on the other side of the earth's globe."

Gaszynski tries to work some authenticity into the story by attempting to create confusion around Rogowski's name. There was an actual Captain Stanislaw Kotkowski in the Pulaski Legion but it's rather improbable that Rogowski's name was distorted as he claims.

"Everyday more adventurers would arrive from Europe, and all wanted high rank, that is why not everyone was accepted. The fact that Washington gave us such distinctions created much envy among the French who had been turned away. Most angry was Girod who had not been accepted - but as he made a large protestation, yelling and lamenting, he was given some money to see him on his way. Franklin and Deane, seeing us in Paris among Dukes, Marquises and other nobles gave us titles of Count, that the Germans call Graff, turning us into Count Pulaski and Count Rogowski. It is true enough that every noble born in Poland is a candidate for the crown, thus having a greater potential than the highest of the nobles abroad - so we let them give us these titles after they learned about our abilities. Pulaski's name gave the Americans little trouble in pronunciation, but mine they just could not manage, twisting it around and calling me Kokoski, or Kolkoski, but never Rogowski."

The memoir ends with a detailed description of Pulaski's desperate charge in the Battle of Savannah, and it's sad consequences.

"Pulaski saw that there was an open space between the redoubts and decided to take a small unit of Georgia cavalry and break through there; get into the city and divert the enemy in this way. General Lincoln praised his bold plan. So calling on the help of God, Pulaski shouted *forward* and we, about two-hundred horse, followed him, galloping so that the earth thundered.

The first two minutes went excellently well, we sped onward to perdition, but with grace, like noblemen. Only when we passed the two batteries between which the gap existed, we were halted by cross-fire and the entire group went into confusion like water that flowed quickly until it hit a closed sluice gate. I look - oh! Painful moment never to be forgotten! - Pulaski is on the ground. I raced over and dismounted rapidly, running to him, thinking the wound may be minor. But here was a great tragedy! A cannon ball had ripped his leg, and from his chest blood was also pouring forth, from another hit. When I knelt and started to raise him, he said with a deathly voice, "Jesus, Mary, Joseph." I heard nothing more nor did I see anything else for in that moment a musket ball slid along my skull, blood blinded me and I totally fainted. Our kind soldiers, urged by Jerzmanowski, retreating toward our lines bore away Pulaski and me (despite a lively fire), as well as other wounded. In the evening, after being bandaged by the medic, I regained consciousness, Jerzmanowski told me that Pulaski lived for yet another hour, but spoke deliriously as the ill are wont to do in fever - about Poland, about the future, and about someone named Franciszka! ... He asked that a cross with the figure of Jesus crucified be handed him, which he kissed and gave up his soul."

While the episode is brilliantly told, it does not square up to the known facts. Pulaski was struck in the groin by a grapeshot. He was not dismembered and lingered for several days before dying of gangrene.

Despite, or perhaps because of, the historical inaccuracies and fanciful episodes such as the meetings that Pulaski had with Franciszka Krasinska and Tadeusz Kosciuszko the book makes for splendid reading. It is imaginative and full of detail. One is almost sorry that the version of Pulaski's story as written by Gaszynski is not the real version. In its own way this work has acquired a historical significance, so much so that Edward Pinkowski had commissioned an English translation. Some of the linguistic flavor was lost but overall, it retained the sense of a folk spun adventure story.

This book should be appreciated for the fiction that Konstanty Gaszynski created in his imagination. It is just one part of the ever evolving and fascinating history-legend associated with a well loved Polish-American hero.

National Shrine of Our Lady of Częstochowa

Casimir Pulaski – A Short Biography

Casimir Pułaski was born on March 6, 1745, in the family manor house near in Warsaw, Poland as the second eldest son of Marianna Zielińska and Józef Pułaski. Józef Pułaski who was an official of the Crown Tribunal and Starosta of Warka.

Pulaski was sent to the court of Carl Christian Joseph of Saxony, Duke of Courland in 1762 as a page. The duke was a younger son of the Polish King, Augustus III. He spent six months at the ducal court in Mitau at a time when Catherine II of Russia sought to remove the Duke and Russian forces occupied the area. He then returned to Warsaw, and his father gave him the village of Zezulińce, from which Pulaski used the title of Starost of Zezulińce.

Having taken part in the 1764 election of the new Polish monarch, Stanisław II Augustus, with his family, he became disillusioned with the direction the new king was leading the nation. At that time, nobles of the Polish-Lithuanian Commonwealth had the right to create "Confederations" to oppose perceived wrongs the king may have committed.

In December 1767, Pulaski and his father became involved with the Bar Confederation, which claimed King Stanisław was a Russian puppet and it sought to curtail Russian hegemony over the Commonwealth and Russian units within its borders. The Confederation was actively opposed by the Russian forces stationed in Poland. Pulaski recruited a unit and, on February 29, 1768, signed the act of the confederation, thus declaring himself an official supporter of the movement. On March 6, he received the rank of colonel (pułkownik) and commanded a unit of cavalry known as a "banner" (chorągiew), which was less than a regiment but more than a squadron. Pulaski actively recruited among the Polish military forces and successfully convinced some forces to join the Confederates.

After some initial victories, his units were forced to retreat to the monastery at Berdyczów where royal forces laid siege to him. After two weeks he was forced to surrender and was taken into captivity by the Russians on 16 June. As was sometimes common during the period, he pledged his parole – which meant he would no longer take part in the conflict and seek to convince the Confederates to end their hostilities.

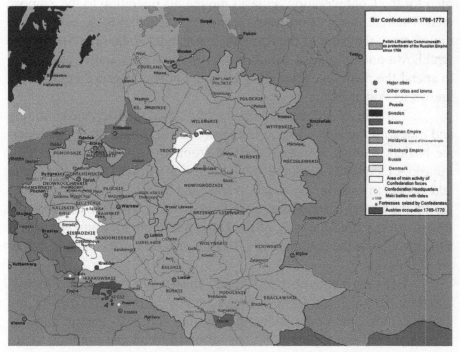

Operations in Poland during the Bar Confederation, Wikipedia

Although he considered this pledge as non-binding, some within the Confederacy sought to court-martial him.

In 1769 he operated in western Ukraine, opposing Russian troops and by April 7, he was made a group commander of the Confederacy in the Krakow area with the rank of Regimentarz. He was criticized by some Confederates for his operations causing him to move with 600 men to operate in Lithuania where he was able to recruit 4,000 men for the Confederation. Pulaski moved his operation to the Zamosć area. The inferiority of the training and experience of these soldiers led to defeats at the hand of the Russian commander Alexander Suvorov at Orekhowa and Włodawa which broke up his forces and required him to spend the next year rebuilding his units in southeastern Poland area known as Podkarpacie.

Early in 1770 Pulaski helped to put down the Bierzynski mutiny and met with the Holy Roman Emperor Joseph II with other Confederate leaders seeking increased support from Austria. Shortly after this, Pulaski's camp was captured by Johann von Drewitz, forcing him to take refuge in Austria. By September he and Michał Walewski captured the monastery at Jasna Gora, near Krakow as a base for Confederate forces. At this time the wife of the Duke of Courland, Franciszka Krasinski, who was the daughter of a Polish noble family, became a protector of Pulaski.

Between September 1770 and January 1771, he helped to successfully defend Jasna Gora from assaults by Johann von Drewitz, but discord among the commanders limited his ability to pursue him. By February 1771 he began operations around Lublin and winning victories at Tarło and Kraśnik. By March, he became a member of the Confederates' War Council.

In May, his refusal to coordinate operations with the French Military adviser Charles Dumouriez around Zamosć against Alexander Suvorov resulted in a defeat of Confederate forces at Lanckorona while he defeated the enemy at Majdany. The loss at Lanckorona, however, severely impacted the Confederates ability to operate. By October there was a plan to kidnap the King – some people claiming that he would be killed – which Pulaski was accused of participating in. This led to a backlash against the Confederates, and they were expelled from Austrian territory.

By May 1772, Pulaski had distanced himself from the Confederation leadership and left for Silesia in Prussia. Leaving Prussia, he went to France where he found that he was tried in absentia and sentenced to death, so he left for the Ottoman Empire in the hopes of reviving the Confederate forces for the Ottomans in their war with Russia. The Ottomans were quickly defeated, and he escaped again to France. This death sentence was reversed in 1793 after the efforts of Antoni Pulaski.

After being thrown into debtor's prison in 1775, his friends raised funds for his release and in 1777 he was recruited for service in the American's war for independence. Benjamin Franklin recommended Pulaski to Gen. Washington for service in the Continental cavalry. He arrived at Marblehead, Massachusetts in July 1777 and by August 20 he arrived at Washington's headquarters at Neshaminy Falls. While awaiting his appointment he served as a volunteer at the battle of Brandywine in September, helping to cover the Continental retreat. Later that month Pulaski was appointed a brigadier general in charge of the four continental cavalry regiments.

In October he took part in the battle of Germantown and spent the winter of 1777 to 1778 at Valley Forge. He moved the cavalry in and around Trenton as part of its reorganization. In conjunction with General Anthony Wayne, he conducted operation in Southern New Jersey. Conflicts on his knowledge of English and attempts at discipline resulted in Pulaski resigning his command in March 1778. At Yorktown he convinced General Horatio Gates to support the creation of a "Legion" of 68 lancers and 200 light infantry. The ensuing Pulaski's Legion was mostly recruited in and around Baltimore and by August 1778 it numbered 330 men who had achieved a relatively high degree of training.

In the autumn of 1778, the Legion suffered heavy losses at Little Egg Harbor. That winter he recuperated in Minisink and was sent as part of General Sullivan's expedition against the Iroquois. By early 1779 he was able to convince General Washington to send him to South Carolina. With a much-diminished force of 60 men Pulaski and the Legion arrived at Charleston in May and was almost destroyed in a skirmish.

During operations around Savannah, he led a cavalry attack of American and French cavalry and attempting to rally some of his forces, he was mortally wounded by grapeshot and was taken to the privateer *Wasp*, where he died. There are conflicts in reporting on where he was buried – some sources say it was at sea, others that he was buried near Savannah at Greenwich Plantation. Remains found at Greenwich were consistent with Pulaski's injury and tested for DNA, but these tests were inconclusive.

Casimir Pulaski gathering supporters for the Confederation at Bar. Painting by Korneli Szlegel, 1860

On the Pulaski Trail - Boston to Savannah

Of all the Poles who came to America, few if any, have equaled the status that Pulaski's name has acquired outside his homeland. Within the so-called "American popular culture" there are a large number of names that have become iconic since the founding of this country. In Poland names like Lech Walesa, Boleslaw Chrobry, Karol Wojtyła, and Jan III Sobieski are universally known. Likewise, in America, there is George Washington, Abraham Lincoln, Benjamin Franklin, Theodore Roosevelt (not to mention FDR) and Martin Luther King -- to name but a few examples.

The memory of these individuals is kept alive through public monuments,[1] observances, portraits (often on coins and banknotes), mention in books, films, in the broadcast news and of course through every conceivable electronic social interaction medium so far invented.

In this universe of popularly known personages the name of Pulaski occupies its own niche. And though it may be far from the center of interest and often is not immediately associated with the Polish American Revolutionary War hero – it definitely exists on the periphery of public consciousness.

Pulaski's name and legend stay alive through presence and repetition in the public sphere. Most commonly, a number of place names have been assigned to Pulaski - streets, parks, squares, highways, counties, towns, schools. He has been the subject of serious books, children's books, and even comic books. His name and face appear on brands of furniture, mustard and beer. Such items, popularly known as "Pulaskianna" are collected by John Szuch of Seville, Ohio.

These are but the tip of the proverbial iceberg. He has been variously honored as a hero of the American War for Independence to be the namesake for a US Navy nuclear submarine (now de-commissioned) that went to sea during the years 1964-1994 as the USS Pulaski (SSBN-633).

More recently, he has received the signal honor as to be only one of eight Honorary United States Citizens by act of United States Congress. The bill was signed into law by President Barrack Obama in Nov.

---

[1]The author personally visited all of the memorials and statues mentioned in this article.

6, 2009.[2]

Pulaski has been honored by having his name associated with military facilities (Fort Pulaski in Savannah) and is the subject of many paintings displayed in public places. Some are very stylish representations in a heroic manner, but not all are quite exact depictions of his face. One in particular is more reminiscent of the immensely popular and gifted actor/comedian Mel Brooks than the Father of the American Cavalry and hero of two nations.

The question may be asked "Why is Pulaski so admired in America?" Yes, he fought valiantly in the cause of American Independence and was the *de-facto* "Father of the American Cavalry." But his stay on the American continent lasted only 26 months, just over two years.

It is true that he gave his life for the cause of independence during the Battle of Savannah, but this alone does not make him a hero. It was rather his personality. Pulaski fits the model of the "American Individualist" - he was courageous, self-reliant, a practiced master of horse and arms. For these skills he was much admired - and envied. It is little wonder he became the archetype of future American generals: James E.B. Stewart of the Confederate Cavalry, George Custer of the American Indian wars, and George Patton of the 3rd Army Tank Corps during WWII. In many ways Casimir Pulaski fits the American cowboy ethos - "ride fast, fight hard, die for a good cause."[3]

That is why when Americans learn his story and legend, they immediately identify with and are attracted to him. One recent example of this is Major Douglas Shores of the United States Marine Corps. As a civilian he was vaguely aware that there was such a person as Pulaski -- because streets and, more notably, the Pulaski Skyway - an elevated road in New Jersey, was named for him. But when he received the Olmsted Military Scholarship to study in Poland and learned more about Pulaski, he wrote his doctoral dissertation about the Polish cavalryman.[4]

---

[2]Honorary Citizenship has rarely been granted; only eight people in the entire history of the United States have received it. In addition to Pulaski (2009), two of the others who have received Honorary Citizenship were also European officers who fought for the American side in the Revolutionary War: Marquis Lafayette of France and Bernardo de Gálvez of Spain (2014). The other recipients are: Mother Theresa of Calcutta, Winston Churchill, William Penn and his wife Hannah, and Raul Wallenberg.

[3]P. Obst, "Amerykanski Indywidualista" *Dodatek Specjalny, Nowy Dziennik,* October 7, 2012, Nowy Jork, NY pp. 10-11

[4]D. B. Shores, *Kazimierz Pulaski: General of Two Nations,* self-published doctoral dissertation, 2014 pp. 7-8

USS Pulaski

Fort Pulaski

In this presentation I would like to examine the memorials and mementos connected to Pulaski on what could be called the "Pulaski trail" on the East Coast of the United States. This runs from Boston, Massachusetts, to Savannah, Georgia, passing through all of the original thirteen colonies.

According to tradition, Pulaski disembarked in Marblehead, Massachusetts and then after introducing himself to the command of the American Continental Militia obtained horses to seek Washington in Philadelphia.[5] This is a trip of 503 km (312 m). He traveled by a land route probably using the Boston Post Road to New York City. Parts of this road have been replaced by modern highways; other parts have been bypassed.

A marker was placed at Marblehead in 1989 by the Polish American Congress of Eastern Massachusetts but disappeared some years later. In 2009 it was replaced thanks to Polish Army Veterans' groups, the Town of Marblehead and private contributors.

In Dorchester, an area of South Boston with a substantial Polish population, stands a bust on a pedestal, installed in Pulaski Park by Polish veterans. The bust was dedicated in a grand ceremony with the presence of Boston Mayor John Collins, on Oct. 13, 1963.[6]

Just to the south, in nearby Rhode Island there is an equestrian statue of Pulaski. Providence, RI. This bronze depiction of Casimir Pulaski on horseback is located in Roger Williams Park. It was designed by Guido Nincheri, cast in Verona, Italy, and weighs approximately 5 tons. The granite pedestal is 8 feet tall. It was funded by the Casimir Pulaski Bicentennial Committee and dedicated in 1953.

In the state of Connecticut there are a number of statues. Their installation was initiated by various Polonia groups. Most notable among them is the equestrian statue in the city of Hartford, CT. This equestrian statue is the only Pulaski monument where the horse has both front legs off the ground. Dedicated on July 4, 1976 by local Polonia it is the work of Granville W. Carter. It is located on Main Street.

There are two places dedicated to Pulaski in the town of New Britain - a middle school and a stela in Pulaski Park. In nearby Meriden there is a standing monument with a life size bas-relief.

---

[5] Z. Sułek, *Polacy w Wojnie o Niepodległość Stanów Zjednoczonych 1775-1783,* Wydawnictwo Ministerstwa Obrony Narodowej, Warszawa, 1976, p. 148
[6] L. Dende, (editor), "Boston's Polonia Pays Tribute to Capt. Magnitzky - Dr. Zakrzewska and Casimir Pulaski," *Polonia Reporter* (magazine), New York, NY, Vol. VIII, No. 6, 1963, p. 15

Pulaski Marker in Marblehead, MA

Pulaski Statue in Roger Williams Park, Providence RI

In the town of Stamford there is a roadway bridge dedicated to Pulaski, on Pulaski Street where there is also a community generated outdoor Pulaski painting. A nearby church has a bell with Pulaski's likeness in bas relief.

Moving into the state of New Jersey we encounter the "Pulaski Triangle," three towns with a Polish-American population each of which decided to remember Pulaski with a different monument.

Paterson, NJ - This fine representation of General Pulaski was dedicated on Nov. 5, 1929, and stands in East Side Park. It is the work of Gaetano Federici. It was funded by Polish veterans. Over the years it has endured abuse from vandals, but after a truck toppled the bust from the pedestal it was completely renovated.

Wallingford, NJ - Funded by local Polonia, this bronze bust stands near the center of town and is the work of sculptor Mieczyslaw Partyka. It was dedicated on October 4, 2002.

Garfield, NJ - This is probably the most recent among installed statues. It was dedicated in 2014. Pulaski is portrayed standing, slightly larger than life size. The statue was part of a new park along the Passaic River and was sculpted by Brian Hanlon, of Toms River, New Jersey.[7]

Pennsauken, NJ - Not far from Philadelphia, NJ stands a bronze bust of Pulaski on a tall stone pedestal that was first dedicated in Pulaski Square, Camden, NJ in 1935. During the 1980s it was relocated to Cooper River Park in Pennsauken by the Polish American Congress. Its maker is unknown.

Perth Amboy, NJ - has a stela with metal plaque dedicated to Pulaski, next to a bust of Copernicus. These items are placed in the appropriately named International Park.

One of the major roads running into New York city from the east side of the Hudson River is the Pulaski Skyway, an all-steel construction of multiple linked bridges. It is probably the longest massive monument/civil structure dedicated to anyone in the United States. Opened in 1932, it is 3.5 miles (5.63 km) long.

In New York City's borough of Brooklyn there is Pulaski Bridge, a draw bridge.

A stela with a bronze plaque on Staten Island, NY, is rumored to be the oldest monument to Pulaski and Kosciuszko. Dedicated in 1926 and placed by the Polish-American citizens of Richmond County. Sometime after 1959 the bronze plaque was stolen and later replaced

---

[7]A. Słabisz, "Gen. Pułaski na stałe zawitał do Garfield," *Nowy Dziennik,* June 22, 2014, Nowy Jork, NY

with a much less dignified stone tablet.[8]

Approaching Philadelphia through Bucks County, Pulaski found General George Washington encamped with his army at Hartsville, Pennsylvania, about 20 miles north of Philadelphia. The historic first meeting between Pulaski and Washington took place at John Moland's house which is now a museum maintained by the Warwick Township Historical Society. It is here that he also met the young Marquis de Lafayette and gained his friendship. He brought letters from the Marquis' wife informing him of the birth of their child. An official historical marker gives a brief history of the events at the site.[9]

Moland House - *Gen. Washington's headquarters Aug. 10-23, 1777, during the Neshaminy encampment of 11,000 troops. Here, the Marquis de Lafayette functioned for the first time as Major General at the Council of War on Aug. 21, and Count Casimir Pulaski of Poland met Washington for the first time. An experienced military commander, Pulaski was later appointed Brigadier General of mounted troops and is remembered as the "Father of the American Cavalry.*

As the British were approaching Philadelphia Washington moved his army south and set up a defensive line at Brandywine Creek to the southeast of Philadelphia. Pulaski, who at this time had not yet received an official appointment, accompanied the army as a volunteer. When the wily British General Howe flanked the Americans by coming around their line from the west, Washington was forced to withdraw. Pulaski was instrumental in organizing a rear-guard action and some historians credit him with saving the colonial troops from annihilation.[10] A historical marker was placed to inform tourists about Pulaski's role in the battle.

Casimir Pulaski - *Polish volunteer, commanded cavalry detachment helping to cover Washington's retreat from Brandywine, Sept. 11, 1777. As brigadier general, served Sept. 1777 - March 1778 as first overall commander of the Continental Army's cavalry. He was mortally wound-*

[8] L. Dende, (editor), "Oldest Pulaski and Kosciuszko Monument in Greater New York," *Polonia Reporter* (magazine), New York, NY, Vol. IV, No. 3-4, 1959, p. 9

[9] P. Obst, "Historical Markers Documenting the Polish Contribution to Pennsylvania" in *Forty Years of the Casimir Pulaski Museum in Warka*, Pulaski Museum, Warka 2007 pp. 324-331

[10] D. G. Martin, *The Philadelphia Campaign*, Combined Books, Conshohocken, PA, 1993, pp. 43-76

The Pulaski Stamp issued in 1931

Pulaski Stamp 1979

ed at the siege of Savannah, Oct. 9, 1779.

The army then continued its orderly retreat to Germantown where, because of confusion in the fog and smoke of cannon fire, an opportunity to deal the British a severe blow was lost. Washington continued to withdraw, eventually setting up camp at Valley Forge to the west of Philadelphia. While the men had to content themselves with building primitive log cabins, the officers were quartered in houses that already stood in the vicinity. In 1953 Polish-American historian Edward Pinkowski published a book "Washington's Officers Slept Here" in which he documented the places where various generals had been lodged.[11] This included Pulaski who was quartered in the very substantial stone house belonging to John Beaver. Located just outside the present Valley Forge Historical Park, an area administered by the National Park Service, the house retains its colonial charm, despite the fact that it has been renovated and updated with all the modern utilities. It is currently a private residence.

Pulaski's presence at Valley Forge is noted on the memorial arch located at the center of the park. It is only thanks to Edward J. Dybicz, a veteran of Polish extraction, that the name was placed there.[12] Originally it had not been included due to some oversight, and it took an appeal to then Pennsylvania governor James Duff, to make the correction. Much more generous were the builders of the Washington Memorial Chapel built in 1904 which is also on the site. Among the bronze medallions embedded in the floor to memorialize Generals of the Revolutionary Amy there is also one devoted to Casimir Pulaski.

By the time he arrived at Valley Forge Pulaski had received his commission as a Brigadier General in charge of the American Cavalry. He started training mounted American troops stationed there in the arts practiced by European cavalry units. He did not have much time to accomplish this necessary task. Need for supplies dictated that the mounted unit move out into the countryside and attack British supply columns. In January of 1778 Pulaski moved his unit to Trenton and operated on the east side of the Delaware River opposite of Philadelphia. A marker exists at the place in Trenton where Pulaski stayed with his troops (at Old Barracks, Trenton).

Soon he joined General "Mad" Anthony Wayne in the fighting

[11] E. Pinkowski, *Washington's Officers Slept Here*, Sunshine Press, Philadelphia, 1953, p. 67-75

[12] *The Times Herald*, Feb. 19, 2015, Bridgeport, PA

against the British in New Jersey. Despite uneven odds he was victorious in a skirmish at Haddonfield.[13]

A contemporary report was published in *The New Jersey Gazette*:

> *Though they [the British] knew the inferiority of our numbers, our attacking them with a few light horse at Haddonfield, under the command of Brigadier Count Casimir Pulaski, made their fears get the better of their knowledge. As well as their courage, and happiest was the Briton who had the longest legs and the nimblest heads. Leaving bag and baggage, they retreated precipitately to Cooper's Ferry.*

While still at Valley Forge Pulaski started formulating a plan to form a fighting unit composed of infantry and cavalry, an independent legion -- which later was called the "Pulaski Legion." This idea had to be approved by the Continental Congress, which had relocated to York, PA, as the British occupied Philadelphia. Consent was granted on March 28, 1778. Pulaski traveled there and visited with his friend the Marquis de Lafayette who had been wounded during the Battle of Brandywine and was recuperating in nearly Bethlehem.[14]

Bethlehem was also home to Moravian Order, a protestant religious community of "brothers and sisters." Here the unmarried women, living in a common house, practiced handicrafts. They made a banner for Pulaski. This historic deed is remembered on an official marker.

Pulaski Banner - *While Pulaski guarded this area in 1778, the Moravian women made a banner which his cavalry carried until he died at the Siege of Savannah in 1779. The banner was later immortalized in a poem by Longfellow.*

The banner was of red silk measuring 26 inches square (66 cm) with a surrounding gold fringe. On one side are the letters US and circling these are embroidered the Latin words UNITA VIRTUS FORTIOR (United Valor is Stronger). It is held that this is the first time the letters US for "United States" were used on a banner or a flag. In the center on the ob-

---

[13]P. Obst, "Pulaski w Okolicach Filadelfii," *Dodatek Specjalny, Nowy Dziennik*, October 7, 2013, Nowy Jork, NY pp. 42-43, 45
[14]F. C. Kajencki, *The Pulaski Legion in the American Revolution*, Southwest Polonia Press, El Paso, Texas 2004 pp. 92-93

verse side is the "all seeing eye"[15] (not unlike that in one of the two seals on the US dollar bill) surrounded by a circle of 13 gold rosettes and the words NON ALIUS REGIT (No Other Governs) also in gold.

The ceremony of presenting the banner to Pulaski (if one ever did take place) was beautifully portrayed in a mural in one of the banquet rooms at the Hotel Bethlehem by George Gray in 1937. It shows Pulaski, flanked by two officers, accepting the Legion banner from the Moravian women.

The original banner was stored at the Maryland Historical Society in Baltimore. Over the years the crimson faded to a dull brownish red. In 1976 the Polish Heritage Association of Maryland Commissioned two replicas from the Sister Servants of Mary Immaculate. One was presented to the Maryland Historical Society and the other to the Sons of the American Revolution (SAR). Subsequently the SAR donated their replica to the Pulaski Museum in Warka, Poland (located on the Pulaski ancestral estate).

Pulaski's recruitment efforts for his Independent Legion were centered in Baltimore. Once the legion was formed, he moved against the British at Little Egg Harbor in New Jersey. There, his cavalry was surprised by the well informed British and suffered some losses. A bronze plaque, mounted on a large boulder marks the locality of the battle. After this misadventure the Legion was deployed to protect settlers from native American raids in the vicinity of Minisink, on the Pennsylvania/New York border. During this time (November 1778) Pulaski was full of doubts about continuing his service in the American cause. He even wrote a letter asking General Washington to release him from service. But he quickly hastened to Philadelphia, where the Continental Congress reconvened after the British abandoned the city and withdrew his resignation.

On February 8, 1779, the Legion started its long march toward Savannah and its final battle. However, by then Pulaski had spent over a year in Philadelphia and vicinity. Historian Janusz Roszko writes that while in Philadelphia Pulaski resided at a "Quaker rooming house" on Chestnut Street.[16] However, no definitive proof of his being there has yet been discovered. It is not unreasonable to believe that some record of his stay may yet turn up at some future date.

Pulaski's presence in Philadelphia and vicinity has been noted

---

[15] This Masonic symbol is cited among the evidence that Pulaski was a member of the secret society.

[16] J. Roszko, *Ostatni Rycerz Europy*, Wydawnictwo Śląskie, Katowice, 1983) p. 324

The Pulaski Monument, Baltimore, MD

The Pulaski Bust in the Capitol by Henry Dmochowski

in the already mentioned markers, and in sculptures. The first such, is a medallion with a side profile on the marble rim of the massive Catholic Temperance Union Fountain in Fairmount Park, built for the Centennial Exhibition of 1876. The second is a heroic bronze statue of Pulaski, executed by Sidney Waugh and funded by retired US Army General William F. Reilly. This fine depiction of Pulaski with a rather large sabre was placed on the west side of Philadelphia's Art Museum in 1947.[17] At Pulaski's feet is the stump of the "Tree of Liberty" symbolic of Poland's loss of freedom in the partitions that eventually ended Poland's existence as a county in 1795. Yet, from this stump a new branch springs with new leaves -- the American experiment of a United States.

In the Independence Historical Park complex in Philadelphia is a portrait of the General with a rather large mustache, painted by Polish artist Julian Rys in 1897.[18]

From Philadelphia Pulaski moved to Baltimore to complete recruitment for the "Pulaski Legion" a mixed formation of cavalry and infantry. Along the way in Wilmington, Delaware, there is a triangular park with a bronze plaque dedicated to Pulaski.

Baltimore remembers him with a beautiful large size bas relief monument which portrays Pulaski on horseback charging with his saber raised, as to strike at the enemy. Baltimore also has a street named for Pulaski and a portrait by Stanislaw Rembski that is housed at the War Memorial. A major road leading to Baltimore has been named the Pulaski Highway. The Historical Society has the original Pulaski Legion Banner in its collection.

In Washington, a city that did not exist in colonial times, the United States government funded an equestrian statue to Pulaski. Located on Freedom Plaza near the intersection of 13th Street and Pennsylvania Avenue N.W. is the work of Polish sculptor Kazimierz Chodzinski who also created the equestrian statue of Tadeusz Kościuszko for the city of Chicago. It was paid for by the United States government and was dedicated on May 11, 1910. On the same day a statue of Kosciuszko was dedicated in Lafayette Park, just a few streets away. That statue was funded by Polonia in an effort coordinated by the Polish National

---

[17] A. M. Heller, *Monuments and Memorials of Philadelphia*, Schiffer Publishing, Atglen, PA, 2012

[18] D. Devine, Doris and Karie Diethorn Fanelli, *History of the Portrait Collection, Independence National Historical Park*, Volume 242, American Philosophical Society, Philadelphia, p. 263

Pulaski Statue in Washington, DC

Pulaski Statue in Philadelphia

Alliance.[19]

At the Capitol is a white marble bust of Pulaski sculpted by Henry Sanders Dmochowski. For several years, until 2013 the Poles in America Foundation, started by Polish-American historian Edward Pinkowski, held a commemoration of Pulaski's birthday on March 6 at that site. Unfortunately, limitations imposed by the stringent security requirements at the Capitol, and the unpredictable weather in March, which caused a postponement of the ceremony in 2013, contributed to having the birthday commemoration relocate to Savannah, GA.

On the way to Savannah, one travels through the states of Virginia, North and South Carolina. In Virginia at the city of Williamsburg Pulaski is remembered in a very unique way. Shortly after his death George Washington asked that a club be organized to honor the memory of the Polish hero of the American Revolution. Such a club was organized in Williamsburg VA, one of the oldest cities on the East Coast. The club has survived to the present day. Its membership number is strictly limited to the years of age Pulaski had at the time of his death. The members meet at irregular times on benches located under a tree near the intersection of Nassau and Duke of Gloucester Streets in the historic part of Williamsburg. When new members need to be enrolled, the entire club participates in making the selection. Requirements are that the individual be a good conversationalist and contribute a bottle of Virginia Whiskey as dues.[20]

In addition, the state of Virginia has a town and a county named for Pulaski. Though Pulaski fought to keep the British out of Charleston he is remembered there only with a street name - Pulaski Street.

Possibly the grandest memorial to Pulaski's memory is the white marble column in Savannah, GA in Monterey Square. Its cornerstone was laid during the return visit of Gen. Lafayette to the United States in 1824-25. Lafayette first met Pulaski at Moland House on the Neshaminy Creek near Philadelphia where George Washington's Army was encamped in August of 1777. He acted as Pulaski's interpreter at the council of war that took place during the encampment. It was there that Washington decided to appoint Pulaski commander of the Continental Cavalry.

---

[19] R. Piątkowski, *Pamiętnik Wzniesienia i Odsłonięcia Pomników Tadeusza Kościuszki i Kazimierza Pułaskiego*, Zwiazek Narodowy Polski, Chicago, 1911, pp.. 52-53
[20] W. Kale, "The Pulaski Club," *Colonial Williamsburg Magazine*, April 2013; *see also*, http://pulaskiclub.com

The building of the memorial was preceded by a great ceremony that involved the participation of the local government, military and civilian notables. Most importantly, the action was backed by the Masonic lodges who anointed the stone with grain, oil and wine. Unfortunately, even after such an ostentatious start little work was done. A temporary stone marker dedicated to Generals Greene and Pulaski was placed on the spot and that was all.[21]

The present white marble column was completed in 1854. Designed by sculptor Robert Eberhard Launitz, it is a fifty-four foot shaft topped by a statue of the Goddess of Liberty, that reportedly served as later inspiration for Lady Liberty, the statue in New York harbor. On the base there are bas relief panels which portray Pulaski's fall in battle and the national symbols of Poland and the United States. The fact that this monument is located in Savannah's Monterey Square, not in Pulaski Square, causes endless confusion for tourists who wish to view this magnificent memorial.[22] The monument is also the place where in 2005, Casimir Pulaski's mortal remains were reinterred in a separate crypt covered by a white marble slab.[23]

Pulaski remains an important figure both for Polonia and for America and he still exerts an influence. For example, in 1999 Senator Barbara Mikulski prominently used his name when presenting her arguments why Poland should be a member of NATO. Pulaski might not be with us in person, but his influence continues. His American career has not yet ended.

One could continue to research and find more tributes on the East Coast set up by Americans and Poles as remembrances to Pulaski's life and deeds. One could also write an entire dissertation on the parades which honor the Polish and American hero. Every year the president of the United States issues a proclamation designating October 11 as "Pulaski Day." Polish communities in New York and Philadelphia organize parades. The state of Illinois has made the first Monday of March a legal holiday, when Chicago Polonians parade to honor Pulaski. Another birthday commemoration is the already mentioned observance at the monument in Savannah, GA.

[21] S. J. Idzerda, Anne C. Loveland, Marc H. Miller (1989) *Lafayette, Hero of Two Worlds*, University Press of New England, Hanover p. 137

[22] E. Pinkowski, "General Pulaski's Body," p. 205-214, in Maciejewski, Janusz (editor) *Kazimierz Pulaski in Polish and American Consciousness*, Wydawnictwo DIG, Warsaw 1998

[23] S. P. Bosse, "Comments from S. Paul Bosse" in *Forty Years of the Casimir Pulaski Museum in Warka*, Pulaski Museum, Warka, 2007, pp. 334-337

His image is deeply engraved into the history of America and into the hearts of patriots. He will continue to be remembered because, as an individual, he is relevant to not only to those who respect him as a fighter for freedom but also for the historic ties of friendship between the United States and Poland.

Casimir Pulaski Marker in Georgia

Pennsauken Memorial

Casimir Pulaski at Moland House

During August 10-23, 1777, Washington's army encamped north of Philadelphia, in Hartsville, on the banks of Little Neshaminy Creek. While the troops had to make do with tents and makeshift shelters, George Washington rented a stone house that stood near the stream from John Moland's widow. This is where he made his headquarters and held meetings with his general staff. In this house he had a quiet talk with the Marquis de Lafayette, that henceforth was referred to as "The Great Conversation" by the younger man. After this Lafayette, who lost his parents at an early age, came to look at Washington as a father figure. The Polish cavalryman, Casimir Pulaski, who volunteered to serve in the Revolutionary Army also came here. He brought letters from France for the Marquis, earning both his friendship and gratitude.

After showing much courage and initiative at the Battle of Brandywine, Pulaski was promoted to Brigadier General in charge of the cavalry by the Continental Congress. In 2006 an updated historical marker with the pertinent facts, approved by the Pennsylvania Historical and Museum Commission, was placed near the house. Two bronze plaques, one for Lafayette (donated by Mr. Francis I. DuPont) and another for Pulaski (gift of Mr. Edward Pinkowski) was installed on the walls of the house. The Pulaski plaque is among the first such to bear the correct place and date of birth for the hero of Poland and America: Warsaw, March 6, 1745. This information was verified by Edward Pinkowski and the Polish Academy of Science.

The house survived as a family home into the twentieth century, while enduring various expansions and modifications. In the 1960s, former Bucks County Congressman Jim Greenwood, then a student, shared it with a man who raised turkeys on the property. Later, the house became a biker hangout and started to deteriorate. It was saved from an ignominious end by the Warwick Township Historical Society and slowly restored to reflect its former charm and grace. The work was financed by federal and state grants plus donors who also contributed period furniture and household items. Even now, George Washington would get a pleasant feeling of familiarity inside the home.

The house is a local attraction and a teaching aid for pupils of the grammar and middle schools in the area. There are also frequent visitors who come on the regular days when this house-museum is open. Recently among them was Caroline Kenworthy and her family from Chicago visiting her grandfather Dr. Harry Kenworthy in Bucks County. What seemed to be an ordinary family tourist excursion turned out to be a long remembered historical experience. Some time after Caroline returned to her school in Chicago, located in an area with a large Polish population, she was able to share her experience at the house with her classmates during "Polish Days." When the name of Casimir Pulaski came up in discussion, she stood up and related the story of how, she visited the very spot where Pulaski met George Washington for the first time with her parents, and included other details related to the campsite. Needless to say, hearing about this made Warren Williams, retired teacher and former president of the Warwick Township Historical Society, very happy. It meant that his words of explanation, as a guide at the house, had indeed found fertile ground despite all the distractions that young people are subjected to today.

Warren specializes in telling the story of the house in the eighteenth century and its recent reconstruction. Last year he wrote and published a book for children entitled "A Basket of Pears for General Washington" based on an oft-repeated local story about how, during the Neshaminy encampment, General Washington was presented with a gift of fruit by some local youngsters. This engaging story includes mention of the other historical figures present at Moland House and their significance in the American War of Independence.

Every year in August there is a re-enactment that tries to recreate certain aspects of that long-ago encampment. This includes actor volunteers who don authentic uniforms and arms portraying Continental era soldiers. Their wives enact the roles of the female auxiliary support column without which no eighteenth-century army could function. Tents are set up and various activities and crafts from that simpler time are demonstrated. It is fun and it's educational - it's an encounter with history.

More information can be found on the website:

www.moland.org

Moland House

Celebrating Pulaski in His Hometown

Unlike America, Poland has only three places that have monuments dedicated to Casimir Pulaski: Krynica, Częstochowa and Warka, which is located 60 kilometers south of Warsaw. As it was the location of the manor on Pulaski properties near the Pilica River, it was also the boyhood home of young Casimir. Eventually, after reconstruction from the devastation of World War II, the building became the home of the Casimir Pulaski Museum. It was here that a magnificent statue of Pulaski was installed in 1979, a twin to the one donated by the Polish nation to the City of Buffalo, in New York state.

Every year the statue is the site of ceremonies that mark the birthday (March) and the heroic death (October) of this internationally famous Polish-American patriot and hero. This is the first part of the museum's mission, to maintain the memory of his life and ideals. The ceremonies are attended by the people of Warka among whom are representatives of the Grojec Regional Council which finances and supports the museum, local dignitaries including members of the Polish Sejm, and often members of the Unites States diplomatic service.

In 2007 the museum celebrated its 40th anniversary with the Second International Pulaski Conference that attracted scholars from Poland and America. (Among those present was the eminent Pulaski historian Edward Pinkowski.) This event was an opportunity to premiere a recently completed documentary film made by Jolanta Chojecka, and for a thorough examination of Pulaski's biography, including the newly discovered circumstances of his death and burial after the Battle of Savannah. There was also ample occasion for international organizations to present reports about their recent activities -- present were representatives from the Pulaski Foundation, the American Council for Polish Culture, and the Sons of American Revolution. This fit in well with the second part of the museum's mission, to maintain contacts with American Polonia and the United States.

In recent times the museum has expanded its schedule of exhibitions, hosting an average of four per year. The subject matter varies and often includes local artists and their work or remembrance of historical events that have a connection with Warka. Most memorable

Casimir Pulaski Statue in Warka

was the 2006 display devoted to Stefan Czarniecki's victory over the Swedes in a fierce battle fought on the banks of the Pilica river. For the 350th anniversary of the event a medal was struck, and a special poster designed. Frequently Polish-American subjects are featured. In past years these included the accomplishments of bridge engineer Ralph Modjeski, son of Helena Modrzejewska; and posters issued by American Polonia organizations. This year a special effort was made to commemorate the arrival of the first Poles at the Jamestown colony in Virginia in the year 1608. The current display includes historical maps and photographs of the reconstructed colony where the early colonists dwelled and the glassworks that were an early attempt at starting an industry in the New World. There is also a historically accurate model of the fort which protected them from Indian incursions.

A recent innovation at the museum has been the annual "Vivat Pulaski" - an American style event that is part picnic, part equestrian show, and part rock concert. Held on the Sunday closest to July 4th, the festivities begin at noon with a parade of antique American cars (supplied by individuals and an automotive museum in Otrebusy) that winds its way from the museum to the town square and back. The main event, however, takes place on a long grassy meadow in the wooded park that adjoins the museum. Here mounted riders, including a Pulaski reenactor, demonstrate the type of spirited riding that would have been common among the cavalry of Pulaski's time. Later, there was music and entertainment on the huge stage set up on one end of the field. Those feeling the pangs of hunger were served from dozens of booths which offered a wide array of culinary delicacies. To slake their thirst there were soft drinks and the famous Warka beer made at the brewery in town. Others, who wanted to learn their fill about native American culture could do so in a very authentic-looking native American village, complete with tepees, nested among the trees. This year the stage acts included an Elvis Presley impersonator, stand-up comedy Polish-style and, after sunset, the Theater of Fire - a whirlwind performance of swirling brands and juggled torches. The best, as always, was reserved for last, in this case the very popular musical group "Zakopower," which draws on its Polish mountain roots for inspiration, and Bulecko, its lead singer. On that day an estimated 10 to 15 thousand people made their way through the park - and everyone went away delighted.

Visitors who find themselves in the neighborhood of the Museum are welcome to tour the interior where they can see not only a display dedicated to the life of Pulaski, but to Polonians who had made a positive impact across the Atlantic. In this group are: Ignacy Jan Paderewski, Helena Modrzejewska, her bridge-building son Ralph, actress Pola Negri, singer Marcella Kochanska Sembrich and other notables. It will be a most memorable meeting with Polish -- and American - history. Note: Those who wish to learn more about the museum are invited to look at its website: www.muzeumpulaski.pl - those interested in the film about Casimir Pulaski should look at www.polishcultureacpc.org (and click on the Pulaski film item).

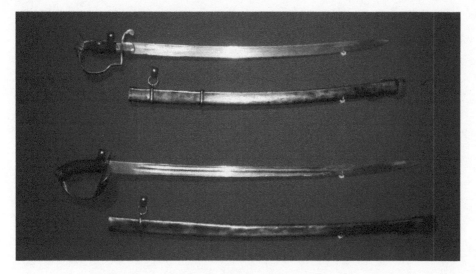

The Cavalry Swords of Casimir Pulaski and Michael Kovats

Pulaski Museum in Warka

"Pulaski The Forgotten Hero"
BY MEL AND JOAN GORDON

(Edited by Peter Obst)

While doing family research, we found a crumbling, tattered letter in an old Bible. In it, a distant grandmother claimed to be the daughter of General Pulaski. Current relatives had attempted to verify this assertion through the National Archives in Washington, DC. The response was inconclusive: while the timing and location of both parties, the grandmother and General Pulaski, made such a union possible, there was no positive proof.

We didn't know anything about General Casimir Pulaski other than there was a 19th century fort[1] named for him near our home in Savannah, Georgia and that he died fighting for America's freedom in Savannah.

Curious, we began our own research. We were soon enthralled by Pulaski, the man, his many accomplishments on two continents, and the rich history of 18th century Poland and America. We found that many people in America and Poland recognized his name but knew very little about General Pulaski. We decided to investigate more and write a book to give him the recognition he deserves.[2]

Our first major discovery appeared to disprove the grandmother's claim. According to people present at the exhumation and examination of General Pulaski's remains in Savannah, Georgia, he was probably intersex, or a hermaphrodite. The bones showed the pelvic and brow form of a female. We went to Warka where church records noting an abnormality at birth seem to support this theory.[3]

Our study of Casimir Pulaski and intersex people accelerated. We consulted Dr. Douglas B. Shore's *Kazimierz Pulaski: General of Two Nations,* Clarence A Manning's, *Soldier of Liberty: Casimir Pulaski,* Antoni Lenkiewcz and Ted Kwiatkowski's, *For Your Freedom and Ours,* Jan Stanislaw's Kopczewski's, *Casimir Pulaski,* as well as

---

[1] Anna Arciszewska, *Fort Pułaski - warto go zwiedzić,* „Nowy Dziennik," Sept. 29, 2016, p. 30-31

[2] Mel and Joan Gordon, *Pulaski: The Forgotten Hero of Two Worlds* (2017)

[3] Charles, E. Powell, editor, *The Pulaski Identification Committee Final Report, 1996-2006*

the film *Casimir Pulaski, Polish and American Hero* by Jolanta Kessler Chojecka, the current Cultural Attache at the Embassy of the Polish Republic in Washington, DC. We also attended conferences and lectures about Casimir Pulaski in 2015 and 2017 at the Kazimierz Pulaski Museum in Warka. We learned a great deal there about the Pulaski family and found a lecture about Casimir's brother, Antoni, especially enlightening regarding the recovery of some of the Pulaski lands.[4]

We also studied books on genetics and intersex people. Among these were *Epigenetics: How Environment shapes Our Genes* by Richard C. Francis and *Born Both* by Hida Viloria as well as other texts by intersex people. In a history of queens and kings we read that Queen Christina of Sweden was most probably intersex and a lecture at the 2017 Conference at the Pulaski Museum in Warka revealed to us that the beloved and well-known track star, Stella Walsh[5] was intersex as well. We consulted medical professionals who told us, like most human traits, dual sexuality is present in varying degrees in many people and some of them are able to reproduce. We noted that the intersex people we learned about were top achievers, like General Pulaski.

Our interest piqued, we traveled to American and Polish battlefields, towns, and churches where Casimir Pulaski lived, worshiped and fought.

The famous Battle of Brandywine[6] in Pennsylvania, USA held two discoveries for us. Although still very new to America and not yet a member of the Continental Army, Pulaski was instrumental in saving the life of George Washington. Without his courageous intervention, America might not be free today. And, ironically, Brandywine Creek flows into the Christina River which is named for Queen Christina, the intersex Swedish Queen of the 17th century.

Early on, we were disappointed that our own Fort Pulaski in Georgia had almost no information available about its namesake. Instead, its museum and bookshelves are filled with histories of the American Civil War that was fought to end slavery. But therein, was another important connection to Casimir Pulaski. The fort named for him

---

[4]Mariusz Kozdrach, *Rozpad fortuny Józefa Pułaskiego (1704-1769)* in Dariusz Kupisz and Andrzej Pytlak, editors, „Kazimierz Pułaski i jego czasy w historii literaturze, kulturze," (2016) p. 51-74

[5]Mary Walton, *Olympic star Stella Walsh: She ran fast - like a man,* "Philadelphia Inquirer" December 14, 1980; also see National Polish-American Sports Hall of Fame: http://www.polishsportshof.com/?page_id=728, accessed January 21, 2018

[6]D. G Martin, *The Philadelphia Campaign,* (1993) p. 43-76

became a safe haven for escaping slaves. Its first Union Commander, Maj. General David Hunter,[7] issued a proclamation that any black person who made it to the fort would be granted freedom. Thus, the fort named for the man who died fighting for freedom continued his mission by helping others find freedom almost a hundred years after his death.

Casimir Pulaski was a great general and an inspirational leader who men followed into battle against much larger forces. An unsurpassed horseman, he became known as the Father of the American Cavalry.[8] He was as fierce a warrior on horseback as any man who has ever lived. He was equally adept at designing effective weapons and colorful uniforms. He often displayed compassion for prisoners and others.[9] He possessed sensitivity, genius, and an analytical mind. We believe that these combinations of male and female traits are indicative of a person who is strengthened by a dual sexuality, being able to draw upon the attributes of both.

Was the grandmother's claim to be his daughter true? We don't know and perhaps never will. But there is some support for her assertion. Most of her descendants have been superb horsemen, as would be expected of relatives of Pulaski. They have also been natural leaders, eschewing the safety of salaried jobs for the higher risk of starting and running their own businesses, joining the military, or pursuing adventuresome careers.

Our admiration for General Pulaski has driven us to tour America and Europe doing presentations and lectures about him. We have been embraced by Poles in America and Poland who, like us, are enthusiastic about gaining the recognition for him that he so richly deserves. We now feel we are Poles, at least in our hearts, and whether blood relatives or not, very connected to General Pulaski, a great hero.

---

[7]James F. Rhodes, *History of the Civil War*, (1968), p. 150
[8]Francis C. Kajencki, *The Pulaski Legion in the American Revolution*, (2004), p. 251
[9]Remigiusz Matyas, *Kazimierz Pułaski: Cena Nieśmiertelności,* (2016) p. 20

Mel and Joan Gordon

Pulaski Commemorations

Casimir Pulaski Day is a holiday officially observed in Illinois, on the first Monday of March in memory of Casimir Pulaski (March 6, 1745 – October 11, 1779), a Revolutionary War cavalry officer born in Poland as Kazimierz Pułaski. He is praised for his contributions to the U.S. military in the American Revolution and known as "the father of the American cavalry".

Casimir Pulaski Day is celebrated mainly in areas that have large Polish populations, such as Chicago, Bloomington, and Du Bois. The focus of official commemorations of Casimir Pulaski Day in Chicago is at the Polish Museum of America where various city and state officials congregate to pay tribute to Chicago's Polish Community.

The city of Chicago celebrated its first official Pulaski Day in 1986. On February 26, 1986, Mayor Harold Washington introduced a resolution to designate the first Monday in March General Casimir Pulaski Day, and the City Council approved. The Chicago Public Library closes in observance of Pulaski Day but Chicago Public Schools remain open. Pulaski Day stopped being a holiday for Chicago Public Schools in 2012 as a way to increase the number of days in the school year, although some Illinois schools still observe the holiday depending on snow days.

This is a separate holiday from the federal observance, General Pulaski Memorial Day, which commemorates Pulaski's death from wounds suffered at the Siege of Savannah October 11, 1779.

Illinois enacted a law on September 13, 1977, to celebrate the birthday of Casimir Pulaski and held the first official Pulaski Day celebrations in 1978. The bill was introduced by State Senator Norbert A. Kosinski, a Democrat from Chicago, and signed by Thomas Hynes, President of the Senate, on June 26, 1977. Cook County government offices, the Chicago Public Library, and statewide public and private schools are closed on this holiday.

Wisconsin public schools also observe Casimir Pulaski Day, although they do not close for it. Banks in Illinois may close for the holiday. Buffalo, New York also acknowledges a "Pulaski Day," which is held in the middle of July, and is celebrated with an annual parade.

Pulaski Day Celebrations with the Pulaski Cadets

Pulaski Day in 2017

On November 6, 2009, President Barack Obama signed a joint resolution of the U.S. Senate and House of Representatives making Pulaski an honorary American citizen, 230 years after his death. He is one of eight people to be granted honorary United States citizenship.

Grand Rapids, Michigan hosts a "Pulaski Days" celebration annually on the first full weekend of October in recognition of General Pulaski and the Polish culture in general.

Pulaski Day Parades take place in several cities including New York, Philadelphia, Chicago and Milwaukee.

Pulaski's birthday is celebrated annually in Savannah in Monterey Square, location of a tall marble column that memorializes the hero of two nations. The sounds of fife and drum and a color guard composed of the Knights of Columbus in full regalia carrying flags of the United States, Poland and the State of Georgia usually open the ceremonies. Along with them, providing the marching music are members of the Costal Heritage Society, dressed in Revolutionary War uniforms complete with muskets. They are usually followed by wreath carriers from the committee. The national anthems of Poland and the United States are sung to the accompaniment of a trumpeter. This is followed by topical remarks from Savannah Mayor and State Representatives. This is accompanied speeches from eminent historians. Then wreaths from the Poles in America Foundation, the American Council for Polish Culture, the Savannah Gen. Pulaski Committee, the Polonia Club of Korona, Florida and descendants of the Puałski family of Puałzie, Poland now living in Greenville, S. Carolina, were placed at the monument. On command, a musket salute was fired in honor of Pulaski's sacrifice on the Savannah Battlefield.

Mr. Edward Pinkowski provided the inspiration for the Pulaski Birthday observance, and the Poles in America foundation was a major sponsor of the ceremony. Mr. Pinkowski did a great deal of research into the life of Casimir Pulaski and augmented what we currently known about the general.

On the 238th anniversary of the battle, three stone tablets were dedicated for Polish-born heroes of the American Revolution: Gen. Tadeusz Kosciuszko, Gen. Casimir Pulaski and Capt. Jan Zielinski. Kosciuszko was a military engineer who planned defensive fortifications at Ft. Mercer, West Point and the victorious battle at Saratoga. He later returned to Poland and led an insurrection (albeit unsuccessful) to wrest the country from the clutches of the occupying powers of Austria, Prussia and Russia. Casimir Pulaski fought for Polish independence as a cavalry commander in the Bar Confederation. He later he came to America and organized Washington's Continental Cavalry. Ultimately, he laid down his life for the cause of American freedom at the Battle of Savannah. Capt. Jan Zelinski was Pulaski's cousin who led a cavalry unit during the battle of Charleston and eventually died from the wounds he received.

During this same weekend Pulaski's birthday is also observed at the Pulaski Museum in Warka, Poland. Wreaths are laid at the statue of Pulaski which is a twin of the one found in the city of Buffalo, NY.

It should be remembered that Pulaski was born on March 6, 1745 as indicated by records at the Church of the Holy Cross in Warsaw where the baptism took place. These were discovered by Slawomir Gorzynski in 1992 and later incorporated into an updated entry for Pulaski in the *Polski Slownik Biograficzny,* an official source for biographical sketches of famous Poles.

The Poles in America Foundation (www.poles.org) and the American Council for Polish Culture (www.polishcultureacpc.org) invite interested parties to view additional information presented on their respective websites.

Pulaski reenactor at a Pulaski Day celebration

A Pułaski Play is Over 100 Years Old

The play, *Casimir Pułaski in America* (A Drama in 5 Acts) written by Adolf Nowaczyński is over 100 years old. Adolf Nowaczyński (1896-1944) was a prolific author who wrote in Kraków and associated with the Young Poland Movement but was never part of the literary establishment. His sharp pen and blunt words tended to provoke violent opposition. He satirized the Sanacja government in the inter-war period and was thrice beaten for expressing his views. During WWII he was arrested and maltreated by both the Gestapo and the Soviet Security Services. Not much is known about the stage history of *Pułaski in America.* When the play was published by the "Ostoja" publishing house in Poznań, the text was reviewed by Zdzisław Dębicki in "Kuryer Warszawski." Dębicki praised the novel approach that Nowaczyński used to portray Pułaski but did not wholeheartedly endorse the demystification of the Pułaski legend. Nowaczyński gave his audience a much different Pułaski than was presented in popular writing.

This was a thoughtful Pułaski who does not rush blindly into battle, somewhat conflicted as to the circumstances he found in the New World.

The style of the play-script is unusual. Each act is preceded by a lengthy description of the place where the action is set. The author goes to great lengths to set the atmosphere for the scene, even describing events that are taking place offstage. In this way it is more like a screen treatment written in preparation for making a film. What is also interesting is how Nowaczyński juxtaposes real historical figures, introduces fictional ones, maneuvers them into new positions and changes the pace of events to suit his purpose. It is obvious that he drew inspiration from the fictional *Journals of Maciej Rogowski* (Konstanty Gaszyński) to flesh out his characters. The Poles in the play (Pułaski, Zielinski, Chotkowski, Benyowsky) use noble-sarmatian expressions like "dalipanku," "egzercyki," "manewracje," "awanposta" and Latin phases to excess.

Act 1

The scene is the interior of Independence Hall, in Philadelphia, where Washington's officers are planning their campaign. Outside a band plays "Yankee Doodle" to which the author supplied new and original Polish words. Among the officers are MacMoyler (a Colonel in the Quartermaster Corps), Zielinski, John Sullivan, Benjamin Lincoln and the Marquis de Lafayette. MacMoyler's flirtatious wife Denise arrives and seems to have an eye for Zielinski. A negro character named Black polishes pistols while the generals and other staff officers' bustle about. During the conversation Tadeusz Kosciuszko is mentioned and praised for his attempt to warn the commander of Ft. Ticonderoga about the possibility of the British being able to place cannon on Sugar Loaf hill which would then force surrender of the outpost (which happened). Pułaski arrives still wearing his Bar Confederation uniform and a Turkish coat. There is a brief reunion with Zielinski. Pułaski states that he is in America to remove the stigma of regicide of which he was accused. Two "sisters" - Angelica and Marta - of the Moravian Brethren arrive to protest the violence and seizures of supplies perpetrated by Chotkowski in the Bethlehem area. Gen. Lincoln reads dispatches brought by couriers. Generals Gates and Arnold have stopped the British advance down along the Hudson River. Kosciuszko is credited with placing the defenses around Saratoga. Americans inside and outside the building begin celebrating wildly. A second dispatch states that Pułaski is appointed to lead the American Cavalry. Pułaski promises that he will not disappoint his commander. Then the bell of Independence Hall begins to toll and the band strikes up Yankee Doodle.

Act 2

The action takes place in Hyphen's Tavern situated on the road from Philadelphia to Chester. The appearance of the interior is described in great detail. The Tavern Keeper and his wife talk about the meager money they are making off the American officers staying there, and that the British are far better customers. Denise and Zielinski arrive, apparently for an illicit secret tryst. Chotkowski comes in, out of the rain. He has left his post without orders and complains about Pułaski's strict discipline and training. General Washington, with Generals Arnold, Knox, Lincoln, and Col. MacMoyler arrive with other high-ranking officers for a council of war. Washington announces that the French will now be supporting the revolutionary cause. Cheers erupt. Pułaski comes and warns the group that the British are three hours march away, passing through the position that Chotkowski left unguarded. He sees Chotkowski and threatens to have him court-martialed. It is discovered that the Tavern Keeper is spying for the British. Soldiers prepare to burn the tavern as Pułaski orders that the spy be hanged from the nearest tree. The act ends as the hapless spy is dragged outside.

Act 3

Pułaski is visiting the wounded Lafayette in Bethlehem at the Sisters' House of the Moravian Brethren. Benyowsky is with him. Zielinski is also there recuperating. They talk about the newly founded Pułaski Legion. Brother Nataniel of the Brethren enters and there is a discussion about the Moravians' pacifistic ways and whether there can be a just war. Pułaski mentions that Chotkowski was killed by the Indians. Sister Angelica enters and Pułaski becomes aware that she strongly resembles his love, Franciszka Krasińska, in Poland. Gen Sullivan announces that the southern city of Savannah has fallen to the British. Denise, repenting her earlier behavior, is now "Sister Denise" of the Brethren. She enters with an embroidered banner the women had made for Pułaski's legion. Sister Angelica makes an oration while presenting the banner. The Sisters are going to accompany the Colonial Army and serve as nurses. Children with flowers surround them singing and the group forms a tableau.

Act 4

The action is set on a hilltop within the American camp outside of Savannah. It is before sunrise and troops are preparing for an early morning attack. There is a tent and a cot on which lies Benyowsky, ill with fever. Pułaski, Gen. Lincoln and Admiral d'Estaing are there. Pułaski tries to convince the other commanders that they should postpone the attack until reinforcements from Charleston can arrive. Lincoln tells him it's too late to change plans while the Admiral accuses him of "Polish insubordination." Pułaski defends himself and his countrymen and agrees to do his duty. Zielinski remains with Benyowsky and they talk about the time of the Bar Confederation. Benyowsky is critical of the Bar leaders especially the firebrand Father Mark whom he describes as a comfort loving fat cleric. A British spy is discovered prowling around the camp. The attack on Savannah begins offstage. Later, Pułaski is carried in on a litter. Sisters Angelica and Denise tend to his wounds, but to no avail as he has been struck close to the heart. News reaches them that Gen. Benedict Arnold had turned traitor. A full retreat begins. Soldiers pick up military supplies and Pułaski is carried offstage.

Act 5

The final act takes place on the deck of a ship, the *Wasp* which is heading for Charleston. Three sailors - Tommy, Bob and Jack - are on deck. Tommy is sewing up the canvas wrapping around Pułaski's body. Two American Indian prisoners with chains on their ankles are washing the deck with stiff brushes. The sailors converse about what happens to a body after it is buried at sea. Then talk turns to their Indian prisoners whom he calls "cannibals" and "redskins." Jack wants to take revenge on the Indians for alleged murders of his family members. He is stopped by Sister Angelica who shames him for attempting to harm defenseless men. The ship's Captain, Gen. Lincoln, and Admiral d'Estaing come on deck to perform last rites over the body. An enumeration of Pułaski's battles and deeds is part of the oration. Information is given that Benjamin Franklin has been sent to start peace negotiations with the British. The Star-Spangled Banner and the Pułaski Legion banner are presented. As a sailor announces that Charlestown has been sighted, the body is lowered into the sea.

Nowaczyński wrote this play just before Poland recovered its independence in 1918, while the Great War was coming to an end. Some of the universal themes connected with conflict: the cruelty of war, blind obedience to orders, and maltreatment of prisoners appear prominently in this play. One may wonder why the character of Black, symbolic of the slavery issue, is introduced in the first act, and then never appears again. Yet the author devotes a major part of the last act to the question of the Native American, those who sided with the British, who are going to suffer because they happened to be on the wrong side of history.

As the centennial of Poland's independence approaches, Iwona Stefaniak, director of the Pułaski Museum in Warka expressed interest in this play and stated a desire to convince some theater group to put on a performance. This will not be an easy task, but by coming to grips with this text we may learn a lot more about Nowaczynski's motivations and draw out the conclusions that he intended to convey.

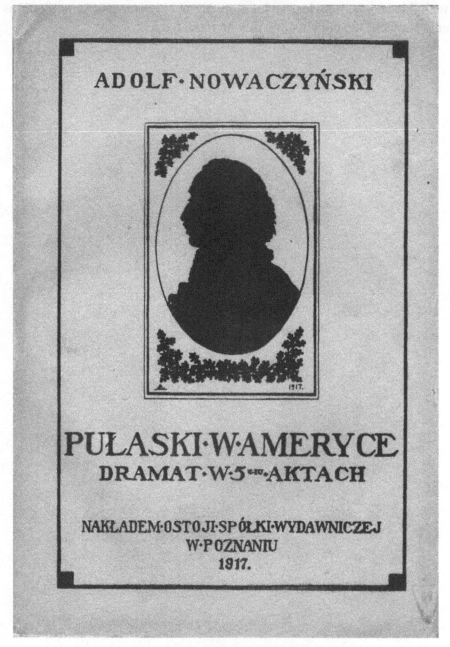

The cover playbill of the Pulaski play from 1917

Not for Children Only

Mention of Casimir Pulaski's participation in the War of the American Revolution is only briefly noted in American textbooks when he is mentioned at all. Yet the cavalry general's reputation as a courageous soldier makes him a natural subject for true stories of adventure. So it is no surprise that twice he made an appearance in that most American of all literary forms -- the comic book, or "graphic novel" format as it is called these days.

The first time Pulaski appeared in a comic book was in 1942 as part of the series "Real Heroes." Distributed widely to the United States Armed forces these books served to entertain and inform. The inspirational and easy to read stories were intended as morale boosters for soldiers. Pulaski's story was included along with those of Sgt. York, John Paul Jones, and Nathan Hale.

Another comic book that featured Pulaski was the "Treasure Chest Series" that were intended for use in Catholic primary schools. Issued in 1961, Pulaski's segment stressed his Catholic background, as many of the American Revolutionaries were Protestants or Free Thinkers. It did not omit, however, a brief reference to his defense of the fortified monastery at Częstochowa, one of Poland's most revered shrines to the Blessed Mother. Another panel had Pulaski praying in uniform at a Catholic church in Baltimore.

Both versions concentrated on the American Revolution, mostly skipping over or summarizing the Polish-American hero's experiences in Poland and the Bar Confederation. Some of the facts, specially the date of his birth and the circumstances of his death were given incorrectly, as at the time those precise details were not yet known. They had only come to light through research done by scholars in Poland and Edward Pinkowski in the United States.

That is why the Pulaski Museum in Warka, Poland, after the current renovation of its buildings is completed, plans to issue an up to date version of Pulaski's biography in the "graphic novel" format. This comic book will serve to entertain and educate a whole new generation of children. It will not be the first comic book in which the museum was involved. It cooperated with a Warka promotional organization to produce attractive comic books. One is based on the 400th anniversary of

Cover of "Real Heroes"

the battle where Stefan Czarniecki was victorious against the Swedes in 1656, and another on Piotr Wysocki, the local hero of the 1830 November Uprising.

However, for those who can't wait, and would like to educate their school age children about Pulaski there is an excellent book in English written with the younger readers in mind. It is called "Count Casimir Pulaski" and in a straightforward fashion tells of the life and exploits of the Polish-American hero. It is nicely illustrated with color pictures and, best of all contains the most accurate facts. This includes the date of Pulaski's birth (March 6, 1745) and his death and burial on land, not at sea as was commonly believed. The circumstances of his final hours were discovered by historian Edward Pinkowski and verified when the crypt under Pulaski's monument in Savannah was opened in 1996 and the General's remains found in an iron box.

The author of the above mentioned book which came out in 2005 (Power Plus Books, New York) is by Ann Marie Kajencki, the daughter of Francis Casimir Kajencki, an eminent historical writer. His definitive work on Pulaski is,"The Pulaski Legion in the American Revolution" (2004, Southwest Polonia press, El Paso, TX).

For those who would prefer to view rather than to read Pulaski's story there is an excellent DVD "Casimir Pulaski - Polish and American Hero" released in 2007 by Jolanta Kessler-Chojecka. The film includes all the latest discoveries about Pulaski and contains interviews with historians Edward Pinkowski and Francis C. Kajencki. Recorded on DVD in a US-compatible system, it has a Polish and an English language soundtrack.

To obtain a copy see: www.polishcultureacpc.org/Pulaski

Casimir Pulaski from the "Treasure Chest Series"

The Pulaski Comic

Recently the Pulaski Museum in Warka was able to realize one of its planned goals which was to publish a comic book on the Hero of Two Nations, Casimir Pulaski. The soft cover book is thirty-six pages long and is entitled "Casimir Pulaski: the Price of Immortality." On the cover Casimir is astride a galloping horse, the background is a dark red. This title opens the question whether Pulaski actively sought immortality through glory on the battlefield? I'd like to think that his motivations were more altruistic, that he only desired to fight for freedom for both America and Poland. He died on that battlefield in Savannah, was recognized for his bravery and passed into history and legend.

This is the first time the entire story of Pulaski's life is told in a comic book, or as some would prefer the graphic novel. There have been some American comic books that portrayed portions of Pulaski's military campaigns in America, but these treatments were no more than twelve pages.

Drawings for the book were executed by Jacek Przybylski. Persons who have seen earlier comics done by Jacek for the Museum in Warka know that he is an outstanding artist who is a master of the graphic comic-book medium. The figures are crisp and contrasting and stand out. The inner pages are all done in black-and-white because of limits on the museum's budget. However, the panels are a pleasure to look at and explore. Jacek did an outstanding job of portraying the emotion on people's faces, and he brought Franciszka Karsińska, the main female character, to life. This great Polish beauty of the 18th century is graceful and strong figure quite reminiscent of her portraits.

If one were to find fault with the excellent draftsmanship of Jacek Przybylski, I would have to say that he made General George Washington too much like the picture on the one-dollar bill. During the Revolutionary War Washington was a younger man but this can be forgiven since the American comic book also use this convention. The other problem is due to the lack of color. The British soldiers' uniforms are similar in appearance to the American ones, so in some frames it is difficult to tell friends from enemies. Had there been color this would not have been a problem since the Americans wore blue and the British preferred red. Overall, however, Jacek delivered a solid job, great action

and beautifully portrayed characters.

As for the script written by Dr. Remigiusz Matyas, it has many fine features showing that he could probably hold his own as a Hollywood screenwriter. The story begins with Pulaski wounded on the battlefield in Savannah and then flashes back to the moment of his birth and childhood.

The Casimir Pulaski presented in the script is a rather conflicted and unsure of himself. He agonizes over the oath he gave the Russians, not to fight again, to assure his release after he was captured after the battle over Berdyczów. Later he feels guilt when his older brother Francis is killed coming to his aid. In other episodes he seems easily manipulated and tricked. This is how the author imagines Pulaski.

Then borrowing a page or two from Harlequin Romance writer Barbara Cartland he introduces Franciszka Krasińska, wife to Prince Charles of Courland, as the romantic foil to Pulaski. While many letters passed between them, and Pulaski visited her even under difficult circumstances, there is no definitive proof of an intimate personal involvement. It must be mentioned that Franciszka and her family were leading figures in the Bar Confederation, where Casimir was a commander. At this point the author lets loose the reins of imagination in constructing a romantic story set among historically accurate events. In one frame we see Casimir with his arms folded in suppliant prayer. A few frames away they are wrapped around Franciszka's waist. Apparently, he prays before the figure, but has the devil under his skin. She gives him an embroidered handkerchief, as was common for ladies to give to their chevaliers.

The story progresses through the episode where Bar Confederates attempt to seize King Stanislaw August. While Pulaski wasn't even there, Franciszka teases him with "I never ordered you to kill the king. You were supposed to kidnap him!" To which he replies, "Yes, truly, I should have abducted you!" Apparently, in this fictionalized version of events Franciszka had quite a lot of influence over Casimir. From documents we know she convinces him to end a feud with Jozef Zaremba, another Bar Confederation commander.

After this we see no more of the lovely Franciszka as Pulaski has to leave Poland never to return. After a brief episode in France and a meeting Benjamin Franklin, he fights on the American battlefield. Wounded, he is placed on the brig "Wasp" and lingers while Paul Bentalou watches over him. In a melodramatic cliche on the final page he clutches the embroidered handkerchief, utters Franciszka's name, and dies.

A panel script explains that a controversy exists as to where Pulaski was buried. One version states that the ship sailed before Pulaski died and therefore his body was buried at sea. The other is a burial on land.

So ends a story set on a historical background and an exciting comic book that my be enjoyed by young and older readers. An English version is planned for the near future. Check the Pulaski Museum in Warka website: *www.muzeumpulaski.pl*

It should be noted that research conducted by Edward Pinkowski supports the version of Pulaski being taken from the ship and dying on Greenwich Plantation. The remains were then transferred to Pulaski's Monument in Savannah GA before it was completed in 1855.

In 1996 while the monument was undergoing renovation an iron box with a silver plate engraved "Brigadier General Casimer Pulaski" was found. A report by Chatham County Coroner James Metts stated that the skeleton was consistent with Pulaski's known description and build.

Recently Dr. James Pula has written an article attempting to refute Pinkowski's thesis in favor of the sea burial. He claims that the remains in the monument were of "another person." If so, then could he please identify that person.

DNA testing conducted over ten years ago was inconclusive because of the poor condition and contamination in the samples taken from the remains. With continuous improvements in the field of DNA analysis perhaps another attempt at a comparison may be made soon.

Remigiusz Matyjas (born: 1965) Graduated from the University of Warsaw, Historical Institute, with title of Doctor of Humanities. His main interest is research of Southern Masovia history. He has written many articles and books, among others winning the grand prize in the "Najlepsze Mazowia" [Best of Masovia] competition. He is a member of the Commission for History and Tradition in the administration of the Main Polish Tourist Society, cooperates with the Casimir Pulaski Museum in Warka, the Polish Independence Museum in Warsaw and the Masovian Institute of Culture in Warsaw. He lives in Zaborów near Grójec.

Remigiusz Matyjas is the best chronicler of modern times in the Grójec District. His texts are easy to read. He writes much and in an interesting way. His texts may be found in the local press, as well as in scholarly publications. He conducts lectures on historical and regional subjects for the Universities of the 21st Century, but also for Grójec youth in the schools and libraries. He has been recognized multiple times for his work. In private, he is a very humble person and a titan of work - says Iwona Stefaniak, director of the Museum in Warka.

Jacek Przybylski (born: 15 July 1975) - graphic artist comics, illustrator, concept artist, painter.

He started his education in the arts in Bydgoszcz at the PLSP (Government Art Schools). In 2000 he completed studies at the UMK (Nicholas Copernicus University) in Torun, in painting. He was a co-author of the comics publication "Kontra" which appeared cyclically during the years 1997-2003. He was active in popularizing the comics medium in Poland and took part in comics competitions. The year 2010 was a breakthrough year in his career. He created the independent album in the series of war comics "Episodes" - "First to Fight - Defense of the Polish Post Office in Gdansk." In the following years he would create album-comics such as: "Piotr Wysocki - A Hero in the Shadow of History" (Warka, 2011) "Hope, Manhood and Death - The Insurrectionist Spring of the Kononowicz Unit" (Warka, 2012), "I Die for Poland - the Pacification of Wola Zarczycka - 20 June 1943" (2013), "Paintings from the history of Lipsko" (2014), "Christmas Eve in the Trenches - 100 Year Anniversary of the Battle of Łowczówek 1914-2014" (2014), "Józef Mokowski - My Journal" (2015).

In 2016 he drew the comic "Kazimierz Pułaski - The Price of Immortality" and recently "Czachowski's Insurrectionist Tracks in the Lipsko Lands - Bloody Old Man" (2016).

Pulaski's Legion

Pulaski's Legion was a combined cavalry and infantry unit approved on March 28, 1791 that was organized and commanded by the Casimir Pulaski and Michael Kovats de Fabriczy for their service with the Continental Army during the American Revolutionary War. The Legion consisted of one troop of lancers, two troops of dragoons, and 200 light infantry soldiers. According to John Mollo, in addition to the three troops of cavalry there was one company of chasseurs, one of grenadiers, two of infantry (fusiliers) and a 'supernumerary' company totaling 268 men.[1]

Pulaski wanted to organize a unit of lancers when he first arrived in North America, but this was denied by Congress. After being appointed Commander of the Cavalry of the Continental army, which consisted of two regiments, he grew frustrated at what he perceived as American indifference to discipline and drill. This was not helped by his lack of command of the English language. After submitting his resignation to Congress, he pulled it back after discussions with General Washington and organized a plan to create a "Legion" which was essentially a combined arms unit based on his experience in the Poland during the Bar Confederation.

The initial orders outlined that:

That Count Pulaski retain his Brigadier in the army of the United States and that he raise and have command of an independent corps to consist of sixty-eight horse and two hundred foot, the horse to be armed with lances, and the foot equipped in the manner of light infantry; the corps to be raised in such way and composed of such men as General Washington shall think expedient and proper; and if it shall be thought by General Washington that it will not be injurious to the service, that he have the liberty to dispense, in this particular instance, with the resolve of Congress against inlisting (sic) deserters.[2]

---

[1] John Mollo and Malcolm McGregor, Uniforms of the American Revolution (MacMillan Publishing Co: New York, 1975) p. 212
[2] *Journals of the Continental Congress*, 1774-1789, Worthington Chauncey Ford, ed. Vol. X, p.291, https://archive.org/stream/journalsofcontin. Hereafter *JCC*.

With this approval of Congress, Pulaski, who had been in York, Pennsylvania where Congress was meeting since the evacuation of Philadelphia in the autumn 1777, went to Baltimore where he established the official headquarters of the Legion.[3] While the Legion was headquartered in Baltimore, other recruiting sites were established in Wilmington, Trenton, Easton, Albany, Boston and Virginia.[4] Pulaski thought that he was given a free hand to raise, train and employ the Legion as he saw fit.

On April 6, 1778 Congress authorized funds to train and equip the Legion. Due to the devaluation of the Continental dollar and inflation, Pulaski ran short of funds before the Legion was fully equipped and on August 20, 1778 and additional funds were authorized. Congress detailed how the Legionaires were to be outfitted:

> *For each cavalryman and light infantry soldier, one stock, one cap, a pair of breeches, one comb, two pairs of stockings, two pairs gaiters, three pairs shoes, one pair buckles, a spear and a cartouch (sic) box: For each trooper, a pair of boots, a saddle, halters, curry-comb and a brush portmantle, picket cord, and pack saddle.* [5]

Brigadier General Pulaski was given authority to select his own officers. This varied slightly from early war procedures where men often elected officers. As a result his officer corps was mostly foreigners.[6] However, the Legion's rank and file "was composed of representatives of various nationalities: Americans, Frenchmen, Poles, Irishmen, and Germans, the latter (mainly deserters from Hessian mercenary units fighting in the British army) being the most numerous."[7] Aiding him in his recruiting efforts was the designation

---

[3]Pulaski initially intended to call it the Maryland Legion, but in the spirit of most "freikorps" it was known by the name of its founder.

[4] Francis Kanjencki, *The Pulaski Legion in the American Revolution* (El Paso: Southwest Polonia Press, 2004), p. 82.

[5] JCC, X, p.312. A "Portmantle" was a case for carrying clothes on a horse and usually rested at the back of the saddle.

[6]JCC X, 364. The first officer appointments to Pulaski's Legion approved by Congress were "... Michael de Kowatz be appointed colonel commandant; Count Julius de Mountfort, major; John de Zielinske (sic) captain of lancers."

[7]Jan S. Kopczewski, *Kosciuszko and Pulaski* (Warsaw, Poland: Interpress, 1976), p. 129. For a complete roster of the Pulaski Legion, both officers and enlistees see: Richard Henry Spencer, "Pulaski's Legion," *Maryland Historical Magazine*, vol. XIII, pp. 220-226, online at MSA. Maryland.org.). Also Kanjecki, *The Pulaski Legion*, Appen-

that the Legion was part of the Continental Army and therefore would qualify enlistees for both the Continental bounty and any state bounty. The recruits would be credited to the states towards their quotas.[8]

For the next five months, Pulaski and a cadre of officers traveled throughout the Delaware Valley, Maryland and beyond looking for legionnaires and equipment. Fred A. Berg noted the following concerning Pulaski's recruiting methods: "George Washington had allowed Pulaski to recruit up to a third of his infantry from German deserters, but Pulaski recruited anyone who came forward in the true 'freikorps' tradition. There were British deserters among the cavalry, much to Washington's displeasure."

It was at this time that a Pulaski legend was born. It involved the banner of the Pulaski Legion and the so-called Moravian "nuns" or "sisters" of Bethlehem, Pennsylvania. On April 16, 1778 (Holy Thursday), Pulaski, accompanied by his commander of the Legion's cavalry, Colonel Kowatz, attended services at the Moravian church, and again in May.[9] The legend developed that in return for Pulaski's chivalric action of placing a guard at the entrance to the Sister's House to protect it from unruly troops, they presented Pulaski with an embroidered silk banner that became the standard of the Pulaski Legion. The episode was immortalized in Henry Wadsworth Longfellow's poem *Hymn of the Moravian Nuns of Bethlehem at the Consecration of Pulaski's Banner*, in which Longfellow related how this religious order presented Pulaski with a flag in which he was eventually wrapped when he was mortally wounded in Savannah.[10] In reality the Moravian "Sisters" were not a religious order but the unmarried women of the community, and Pulaski commissioned the women to sew a standard. It was not a large flag but an eighteen-inch square guidon described as follows:

The original is at the Maryland Historical Society. The standard is eighteen-inch square with deep green bullion fringe, originally silver and has a sleeve for its staff. The field is made of two layers of crimson silk, (now faded) with emblems embroidered in yellow silk. The obverse side of the flag shows a brown "All Seeing Eye" within a circle

dix F, "Muster Rolls of the Pulaski Legion," pp. 317-339.

[8]https://allthingsliberty.com/2017/08/casimir-pulaskis-difficulties-recruiting-legion/

[9]Fred A. Berg, *Encyclopedia of Continental Army Units* (Harrisburg, PA: Stackpole Books, 1972) p.101

[10]Colonel Michael Kovats de Fabriczy, Hungarian cavalry officer who Pulaski recommended to Washington to be his Commandant of Horse, was killed at the Battle of Charleston, May 11, 1779.

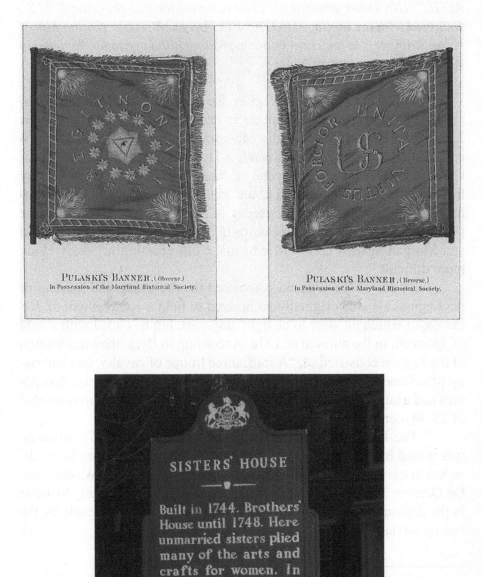

PULASKI'S BANNER. (Obverse.)
In Possession of the Maryland Historical Society.

PULASKI'S BANNER. (Reverse.)
In Possession of the Maryland Historical Society.

SISTERS' HOUSE

Built in 1744. Brothers'
House until 1748. Here
unmarried sisters plied
many of the arts and
crafts for women. In
1778. Pulaski's banner
was made by them.

of thirteen eight pointed stars surrounded by the motto "NON ALIUS REGIT" (No Other governs). ... The reverse side has the letters "U S" encircled with the motto, "UNITAS VIRTUS FORCIOR" (Union Makes Valor Stronger). In the corners are exploding hand grenades depicted in yellow and white thread.[11]

While Pulaski was his legion, the last major battle in the northern theater of operations took place in late June 1778 at Freehold, New Jersey (the Battle of Monmouth). Most sources suggest he was not present, however, Capt. Johann Ewald, a Hessian officer with the Jaeger Corps, placed Pulaski at the scene on June 27 he noted: "About midday the Marquis de Lafayette and count Pulaski appeared; the latter commanded the advance guard yesterday . . ." and on July 2 " . . . that he (Washington) had pushed three corps under Generals Lafayette, Pulaski and Morgan against us in order to make our crossing at Sandy Hook more difficult." [12]

By July 1778, Pulaski completed the recruiting and training of his Legion. He was originally authorized to field a complement of 268 troops, of which 68 were to be light dragoons, but he ended with a total of 330 men, in the autumn of 1778. According to Berg, the organization of the Legion consisted of, "A staff, three troops of cavalry, one company of riflemen (chasseurs), a grenadier company, two infantry companies and a supernumerary company. Each company and troop consisted of 25-30 men."[13]

The Legion was not activated until September 1778 when he was issued initial orders to move on the Hudson River before being directed to move to Princeton and wait for orders by General Washington. On October 3 he was then directed, "...to proceed immediately to assist in the defence of Little Egg Harbor against the attack now made by the enemy on that part."[14]

---

[11]Edward W. Richardson, *Standard and Colors of the American Revolution* (Philadelphia: University of Pennsylvania Press, 1982), pp. 52-53. See page ** of this book for an image.

[12]Johann Ewald, *Diary of the American War: A Hessian Journal,* Joseph Tustin, ed. (New Haven: Yale University Press, 1979), 135. It should be noted that the editor (Tustin) in footnote 54 (403) stated the person heading the "advanced guard" was really Col. Stephen Moylan who took command of the Continental Calvary after Pulaski's resignation.

[13] Berg, *Encyclopedia of Continental Army Units*, p. 101.

[14] *JCC* XII, pp. 983-984.

After all the time and money that went into the forming of Pulaski Legion, neither they nor their Commander fared well. On October 15, 1778 there occurred what has been called the "Massacre of the Pulaski Legion" or "The Affair at Egg Harbor" where approximately forty to fifty Legionnaires were killed by a surprise night attack by British forces led by Capt. Patrick Ferguson at the Jersey Shore. Following this fiasco, the Legion was sent to northwestern New Jersey, the tri-state area on the Delaware River known as the "Minisinks," where Pulaski complained that he had nothing to fight but "bears."[15] At this point Pulaski seriously considered returning to Europe, however the change in the focus of the war to the Southern States where it took part in the siege of Savannah in 1779, and the siege of Charleston in 1780. The Legion's 1st Cavalry was commanded by Maj. Pierre-Francois Vernier during the siege of Charleston's first bloody skirmishes. After Pulaski's death the Legion was broken up. Some sources say the cavalry went to the 1st Light Dragoons and infantry was sent to the 1st South Carolina Infantry. Other sources indicate the remnants were absorbed into Armand's Legion.

The unit was equipped with a cavalry-style dragoon helmet with a short blue jacket and red facings for both infantry and cavalry units. The infantry seemed to have been equipped with overalls and the cavalry with buckskin breeches and boots. The infantry had muskets and possibly hangers (small swords), while the cavalry was armed with sabers, carbines, possibly pistols and as appropriate lances.

[15]Kajencki, *The Pulaski Legion*, p.130

The Memorial for the Little Egg Harbor Massacre, Little Egg Harbor, NJ. On the far right is Edward Pinkowski, on the far left is Henry Archacki.

Pulaski Cadets

At many Polish patriotic celebrations and events related to historical anniversaries an elegant honor guard is often seen - men dressed in uniform white uniforms and shiny black shakos marching with military precision - these are the Pulaski Cadets.

The Pulaski Cadets are registered in Trenton, NJ and are members of The Centennial Legion of Historic Military Commands, but most of them live in and around Perth Amboy, NJ. The organization includes veterans of the armed forces who want to maintain military and patriotic traditions along with the memory of General Casimir Pulaski. This organization is committed to charitable work and has a scholarship program for outstanding students.

The Pulaski Legion was originally formed as a mixed cavalry and infantry formation and operated as an independent detachment during the American Revolutionary War. Half a century later, and with many changes, the Legion was incorporated into New York's 9th Infantry Regiment and took part in hostilities during the American Civil War of 1861-1865. In 1867, soldiers of the Pulaski Legion and other veterans from New York State regiments united to form an organization called The Old Guard of the City of New York.

Almost ten years later, in 1876, the Centennial Legion of Historic Military Commands was formed under Maryland law to bring together existing military units and veterans from past wars. The goal of the Centennial Legion of Historic Military Commands is to keep military traditions alive, record their achievements, conduct patriotic activities, and foster respect for the flag and the US Constitution.

In 1985, the organization of the Pulaski Cadets was established as part of The Centennial Legion of Historic Military Commands, the founder and first commander of which was General Jan Krepe (1985-1990). It resumed operations under the name of Casimir Pulaski. The second commandant was General Ludwik E. Michael (1990-1992), after him Colonel Tadeusz Wieniawa Dziekanowski was elected, serving for 20 years until his death in 2013. He was followed as commandant by Captain John Stroczynski, a former US Army soldier. In 2010, the Pulaski Cadets celebrated their 25th anniversary. In 2017 Captain Stanley Bankowski became the fifth commander.

The cadets participate in many Polish and patriotic events such as the Pulaski Parade in New York and the annual Soldier's Day at the National Shrine of Our Lady of Częstochowa in Doylestown, PA. They were present at the military funeral of General Casimir Pulaski in Sa-

Pulaski Cadets (white uniforms); standing center, from left - Debbie Majka, Peter Obst, Jack Pinkowski, Delores Czaplicki, S. Paul Bosse; (sitting) Edward Pinkowski.

Pulaski's standard carried by the Pulaski Cadets

vannah, GA (2005), They also took part in the celebration of General Pulaski's birthday organized by Edward Pinkowski and the Poles in America Foundation at the Capitol in Washington. Representatives of the United States Congress Dan Lipiński (IL) and Marcy Kaptur (OH) joined them at the ceremony.

When the Cadets take part in parades, they march with the flags of the USA and Poland, also with a specially made large replica of the banner of the Pulaski Legion from 1778. The original of this banner was only a square of 26 inches (66 cm). It is red in color with golden fringes and the words embroidered on it: UNITA VIRTUS FORTIOR (United Valor is Stronger).

Historians remind us that this banner was the first to have large US (for United States) initials embroidered with gold thread. On its back is the "all-seeing eye of God" (as on the seal on the reverse of a dollar banknote) surrounded by a circle of 13 gold rosettes and the words NON ALIUS REGIT (No one else reigns).

In 2014, the Pulaski Cadets served as a guard of honor during the commemoration of the anniversary of the outbreak of World War II, dedicated to the murdered Polish officers and other victims of Stalinism.

More information about the Pulaski Cadets can be found on the attractive website: www.pulaskicadets.org

Pulaski Documentary Film

In October 2007, at the Pulaski Conference in Warka, Poland, Jolanta Chojecka premiered her documentary to the general acclaim of the audience. Taking advantage of the latest discoveries about Pulaski's life and times, hers is the most authoritative and complete Pulaski documentary made to date. Running just under an hour, it manages to present Pulaski's military career in Poland and, in the second half, his vital role in the creation of the United States Cavalry, and his sacrifice for American independence on the battlefield in Savannah, Georgia.

The project was conceived in the year 2000 when Jolanta, an experienced documentary film-maker wrote to Edward Pinkowski, one of the foremost experts on Casimir Pulaski living in the United States, about the possibility of making a documentary film about the *Hero of Two Nations*. Edward Pinkowski handed the letter to his assistant, Peter Obst. A year later when Jolanta came to the states Peter met with her and so started a long collaboration that led through many states and locations. One major problem was funding, another the fact that Jolanta was in the United States only occasionally. Eventually some modest contributions were received from the American Council for Polish Culture, The Philadelphia Chapter of the Kosciuszko Foundation and individual sponsors. At the very end grants from the Polish Ministry of National Defense, Polish TV, and the Film Institute covered the soundtrack and narration costs.

Jolanta was able to place footage from historical re-enactments into the film. She also incorporated interviews given by various historians, including Edward Pinkowski, Col. Francis Kajencki; archivist Fr. Edward Batko and others. She utilized many actual locations of battles to illustrate the story. Historian Colonel Tadeusz Krzastek of the Polish Air Force assisted in creating a factually correct background narrative (in both Polish and English versions), that was combined with an appropriate musical score to accentuate the action.

Though certain incidents had to be summarized, no effort was spared to make the filmed story of Pulaski's life understandable to both Polish and American viewers. Computer animations show the course of events in the important military struggles in which Pulaski took part. Archive footage at the end references the military connection of Pulaski to the Polish cavalry before World War II. The film is a significant achievement in the art of documentary film making, and a fine way to pay tribute to the memory of General Pulaski.

This documentary reflects all the recent discoveries about Pulaski's life including the correct date of his birth which was March 6, 1745. Recorded on DVD in a US-compatible system, it has a Polish and an English language soundtrack.

To obtain a copy see: www.polishcultureacpc.org/Pulaski

The Casimir Pulaski: Hero of Two Nations DVD

Reenactors restage the battle of Savannah

Jolanta Kessler-Chojecka and Peter Obst at the Brandywine battle site.

Indiana Rangers Carbine and Pistol (Photo by the Rocksbury Daily-Press)

Pulaski's Grand Burial in Savannah

In October 2005 there was a Military and Religious Funeral for General Casimir Pulaski. During the seven days leading up to the event, Pulaski's remains, already in the fine white-oak casket that was brought from Poland a year ago, the gift of the Liebchen and Godlewski families, made a tour of Savannah houses of worship. The first stop, on Sunday Oct. 2 was at the First African American Baptist Church where a grand memorial service was held that included the singing of black spiritual music and an oration by the pastor who stressed that Pulaski came to America to fight for the freedom of all. On the days that followed the remains lay in state at the Independent Presbyterian Church, St. John's Episcopal Church, the Mikveh Synagogue and the Unitarian Church. From this last place it would be transported to the Roman Catholic Cathedral of St. John the Baptist for the memorial mass on Sunday.

On Thursday evening a special presentation "Pulaski at Brandywine, PA Charleston, SC and Savannah GA" was made by Ret. Colonel Francis Casimir Kajencki at Savannah's Visitors center. About 300 persons attended the speaker's slide-illustrated lecture which was enthusiastically received. The question session lasted well into the night.

By Friday, most of official visitors had all arrived. The Polish government delegation which had come in from Poland on the Polish Presidential aircraft was headed by Poland's Undersecretary of State Andrzej Majkowski. There were also 12 riders (from a ceremonial-parade unit) and several veterans from the "September 1939 Defensive Campaign." Bishop Tadeusz Ploski, a general and chief of the Polish Army Chaplains, was part of this delegation. Coming from Poland's embassy in Washington D.C. was the newly appointed Ambassador Janusz Reiter and military Attache General Kazimierz Sikorski, and others. Among the last to arrive was a group from Warka, the ancestral home of the Pulaski family, where a museum now stands dedicated to Pulaski's memory. Its members were: Iwona Stefaniak, the Pulaski Museum Director; Miroslaw Maliszewski, Grojec County Administrator (recently elected as deputy to the Polish Parliament); Teresa Knyzio, President of Warka City Council; and Jolanta Kazimierska, Director of the Warka Brewery.

On Saturday while Pulaski's casket was at St. John's Episcopal Church, final preparations were completed at the monument on Monterey square to house the casket for perpetuity. A white marble crypt had been installed in front of the monument and the appropriate landscaping done with red and white flowers. That evening, a banquet was given at the International Trade and Conference Center - Grand Ballroom. This allowed out-of-town participants to meet the distinguished guests from Poland and mingle with local dignitaries. After dinner a number of presentations were made by the Sons of the American Revolution and the Pulaski Cadets honoring individuals for their roles in keeping the memory of Casimir Pulaski alive. Among those were American Council for Polish Culture (ACPC) President Debbie Majka and ACPC First Vice-president S. Paul Bosse. The Pulaski Cadets also presented two replica Pulaski banners, one to the City of Savannah, was received by Francis X. Hayes, and one to Poland that was given into the hands of the Polish Veterans from 1939.

Ceremonies on Sunday Oct. 9 started early. Before the sun had risen, Revolutionary war reenactors and patriotic groups wishing to pay their respects to the fallen in the Battle of Savannah, gathered at the Visitors Center on Martin Luther King Boulevard. From there, to the sound of fife and drum, as the sun began to rise, they marched to the nearby battlefield where a replica rampart had been erected. There, after a speaker recounted the course of the battle, wreaths were placed. A cannon shot sounded in salute to those who like Pulaski, gave their all to the cause of American Independence.

Many of those present then proceeded to the cathedral for the memorial mass. Well before noon, a number of units began to assemble on Abercorn Street and on the steps leading to the church. These consisted of a US Army color guard with flags, a unit of infantry with a squad that was to fire a salute at the grave, sailors from the USS Roosevelt, the Knights of Columbus, the Pulaski Cadets, the Polish riders (5 on horseback), the 1939 veterans from Poland (on foot), and a burial detail (in nineteenth century uniforms) from Arlington Cemetery whose four white draft horses pulled a caisson that held Pulaski's casket. A riderless horse was included to memorialize the fallen General. On arrival, the casket was placed on a catafalque on the steps of the Cathedral where it remained throughout the mass, guarded by sailors from the USS Roosevelt in immaculate white uniforms. Bishop Ploski was the chief celebrant of a memorial mass conducted mainly in Polish, during which both the Cathedral Choir and a Polish Choir from Hamilton, Canada sang appropriate hymns. Then the congregation followed the bishop to the street and joined ranks with the units outside. The procession made its way down Abercorn Street toward the river, then turned onto Bull Street proceeding toward Monterey Square. It was a splendid sight with flags, horses, uniforms and flowers that wound its way over nearly twenty-two blocks.

On reaching Monterey Square the participants of the march took their places and Bishop Ploski began the ceremony of Christian Burial. He was assisted by an Anglican priest, a member of the Savannah Masonic Lodge and the Rabbi from the nearby synagogue. With the casket in the crypt chamber, the solemnities concluded, and a twenty-one gun salute was fired and "Taps" sounded.

Later in the evening the officer and crew of the USS Roosevelt, in cooperation with the Navy League, hosted a outdoor reception on the rear helicopter landing pad of the guided missile destroyer. The Stawski family, importers of fine spirits from Poland, donated several cases of Polish wine to be enjoyed by the guests. A tour of the ship was afforded to all visitors. Commemorative USS Roosevelt plaques were presented to ACPC President Debbie Majka, ACPC First Vice-president S. Paul Bosse and other members of the Pulaski Jubilee Committee.

On the following day a dedication ceremony was held at 10 am. By then the crypt had been sealed with a white marble capstone and the area prepared for the subsequent wreath laying. After the choir from the First African Baptist Church sang, patriotic, city and Polonia organizations paid respect by placing flowers and wreaths on the grave. Pulaski was inducted into the Georgia Military Hall of Fame and the Sons of the American Revolution. The ceremonies concluded with the reading of several proclamations, one of them from the president of Poland, Aleksander Kwasniewski.

Pulaski's Casket being taken to St. John's Episcopal Church by sailors from the USS Roosevelt

Wreaths at the Savannah Battlefield

Pulaski grave in Monterey Square, Savannah, Georgia

About Edward G. Pinkowski

Pinkowski, Edward G. (b. August 11, 1916 to Polish immigrant parents in Willimansett, MA), historian, author, journalist. He was 103 years old and passed away peacefully during his sleep on January 11, 2020 at his home in Cooper City, Florida.

On the occasion of his 95th birthday in 2011 and his 100th birthday in 2016, he was honored by official proclamations from Broward County, Florida and Cooper City, Florida in recognition "as a national authority and among the greatest Polish-American historians of our century."

Among his lifetime achievements, he was responsible for the identification and establishment of the Thaddeus Kosciuszko National Memorial under the auspices of the National Park Service in Philadelphia and the identification and recognition of the final resting place in Savannah, Georgia of Casimir Pulaski, Polish American hero of the American Revolution and founder of the United States Cavalry.

When he was 14 years old, the family moved to the hard coal fields of Pennsylvania, where his father and grandfather previously worked in coal mines of the Mount Carmel area. There he started a writing career while still in high school. During World War II, he was a writer in the U.S. Navy and rose to the rank of Chief Specialist (X).

In 1967 he received the Kosciuszko Sesquicentennial Medal in Toronto from the Polish American Historical Association (PAHA) for locating General Kosciuszko's last residence in America, saving it for the purpose of creating a national monument, and placing an historical marker at 3rd and Pine Streets in Philadelphia. In 1976 the house-museum opened as the Thaddeus Kosciuszko National Memorial under the auspices of the National Park Service.

He was a member of the Philadelphia Historical Commission from 1969 to 1985, and earlier was president, for four years, of the Spring Garden Civic Association in Philadelphia. He was the first lay chairman of the nominating committee and vice president of PAHA. He was chairman of the Ethnic Council and vice president of the Philadelphia 1976 Bicentennial Corporation. He was a founder of the Polish Heritage Society of Philadelphia, an affiliate of the American Council for Polish Culture (ACPC), and the person who created the name of that local organization. He served as a board member of the American Center of Polish Culture in Washington, DC.

He erected a monument at the gravesite and a roadside marker in Douglassville, Pennsylvania to Anthony Sadowski, a Polish American frontiersman, 300 years after his birth. In 1989, he earned the Mieczyslaw Haiman Medal from PAHA "for outstanding Contribution in the field of Polish American studies." In 1997 the ACPC recognized his lifetime of contributions to research in Polish American history by awarding him the Distinguished Service Award.

In 1996 he proved that General Pulaski's remains were buried in a brick vault under the monument in Savannah, Georgia and was recognized by the mayor of Savannah with a key to the city for literally "rescuing Pulaski's body from oblivion." This was documented with DNA evidence in research sponsored by the Smithsonian Channel and broadcast as a documentary during 2019. Over the years, he devoted countless hours to research on Kosciuszko and Pulaski, not to mention hundreds of other figures, and is the author of several books and many articles.

In 2001, Edward Pinkowski was a recipient of the Cavalier's Cross of the Order of Merit (Krzyz Kawalerski Orderu Zaslugi RP) awarded by President of Poland Aleksander Kwasniewski. Among the awards in recognition for his work are the Ellis Island Medal of Honor (2004), the Kosciuszko Foundation Medal (2006), and the Pride of Polonia plaque (2009). He was presented with the Distinguished Service Award from the American Institute of Polish Culture in Pinellas County, Florida (2003). He received international recognition for his work at the Museum of Kazimierz Pulaski in Warka, Poland.

To continue his lifelong commitment and dedication to the Preservation of Polish Heritage in America, Edward and his son, Jack Pinkowski, Ph.D., established the Poles in America Foundation, Inc., www.poles.org. It is a repository of his research and resource materials related to the Polish American experience and contributions to America.

Edward Pinkowski is the author of several books and monographs:

Lattimer Massacre, 1950; (monograph)

History of Bridgeport, Pa., 1951; (monograph)

Washington's Officers Slept Here, 1953; (book)

Forgotten Fathers, 1953; (book)

Chester County Place Names, 1955, 62; (book)

John Siney - The Miners' Martyr, 1963; (book)

Anthony Sadowski - Polish Pioneer, 1966; (monograph)

Pills, Pen and Politics: The story of Gen. Leon Jastremski,1974; (book)

General Pulaski's Body, 1996; (monograph)

Credit for accompanying portrait, Colin Davidson, internationally renowned Irish portraitist.

================

Sources: *Marquis Who's Who in the East 1972-1973*, 13th edition, Chicago, 1972-1973; *Encyklopedia Polskiej Emigracji i Polonii*, ed. by Kazimierz Dopierala, Oficyna Wydawnicza Kucharski, Torun 2005

Edward G. Pinkowski

Index

About the Author

Peter Joseph Obst lives in the vicinity of Philadelphia, PA, USA. He received his Masters Degree from La Salle University where he later was employed as an adjunct lecturer. For over 20 years he has been associated professionally with the Poles in America Foundation, started by Polish-American historian Edward Pinkowski. He researches Polonia history, translates and writes articles. A recipient of Poland's Cavalier Cross of the Order of Merit and the Eagle of the Polish Senate. He is active in Polonia organizations.

BOOK INSTITUTE

©POLAND

This publication has been supported by the © POLAND Translation Program

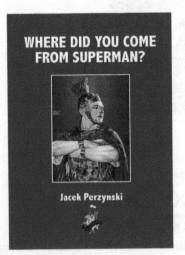